A Friedman/Fairfax Book
Friedman/Fairfax Publishers
Please visit our website: *www.metrobooks.com*

This edition published by Friedman/Fairfax
by arrangement with The Ilex Press Limited
2002 Friedman/Fairfax Publishers
Text © 2002 The Ilex Press Limited

A CIP record for this book is available from
the Library of Congress

This book was conceived, designed, and produced
by The Ilex Press Limited, The Barn, College Farm,
1 West End, Whittlesford, Cambridge CB2 4LX
England*Sales office:* The Old Candlemakers, West
Street, Lewes, East Sussex BN7 2NZ

Publisher: Alastair Campbell
Executive Publisher: Sophie Collins
Creative Director: Peter Bridgewater
Editorial Director: Steve Luck
Art Director: Tony Seddon
Editor: Chris Middleton
Designer: Andrew Milne
Development Art Director: Graham Davis
Technical Art Editor: Nicholas Rowland

ISBN 1-58663-681-2

Distributed by Sterling Publishing Company, Inc.
387 Park Avenue South
New York, NY 10016

Distributed in Canada by
Sterling Publishing
Canadian Manda Group
One Atlantic Avenue, Suite 105
Toronto, Ontario, Canada M6K 3E7

*For up-to-date resources and information on this title,
visit:* www.webexpertseries.com/photoshop

WEB PHOTOSHOP EXPERT

USE PHOTOSHOP TO CREATE
FANTASTIC WEB GRAPHICS

PETER COPE

CONTENTS

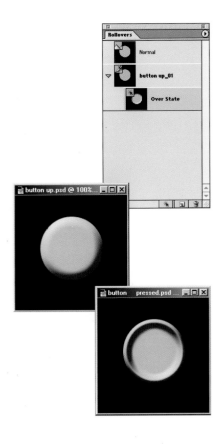

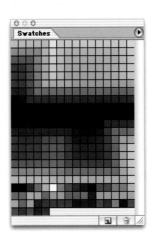

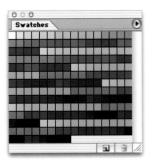

6

Introduction

In the early 1990s, the appearance of Adobe's Photoshop did for photography what the graphical user interface (GUI) did for desktop publishing. Within a few short years, photographers and designers were creating stunning images and graphics. A new, virtual art form had been created. The emergence of the Internet and our voracious appetite for creating and visiting websites has brought new challenges and opportunities for the designer. Photoshop and its newer, Web-savvy sibling ImageReady are ideal for meeting these opportunities—and this book will show you how.

Web Expert Photoshop is packed with ideas and information on how to make Photoshop the ultimate design tool for Web images. We'll look, for example, at how to improve and enhance your photographs and then send them to friends and colleagues over the Internet. We'll also investigate how Photoshop's tools can also be used to create the images and graphics for stunning and unique webpage interfaces—and make the interfaces work on real websites! Most of all, we'll cut through the jargon of the Web and aim straight at creating great artwork.

Everything in this book can be achieved using Photoshop and ImageReady. All the image manipulation projects can also be done using the entry-level version, Photoshop Elements. By following the simple, step-by-step examples, you'll quickly be able to exploit Photoshop's unique power and create artwork for your website that is every bit as good as the professionals'.

At a time when website-building software (of the type that might be given away on a magazine cover disk or downloaded freely from the Internet) can create a website from start to finish, you might ask *Why bother with Photoshop?* That question is even more pertinent these days when you consider that this same, free software can give a professional gloss to a website with just the lightest of touches from the site's creator.

The answer is one of differentiation. True, most software applications will make an effective job of creating your website, but creating a unique and individual interface requires imagination—that will come from you—and the tools to realize your vision. That's where Photoshop comes into its own. Let's set about building websites that people will remember—for all the right reasons!

What Photoshop uniquely offers the website designer is all the sheer image-manipulation power that professional photographers already have at their fingertips, such as powerful filters and special effect-generating tools, combined with an artist's box full of infinitely modifiable brushes and drawing tools. All this intuitive and inspirational technology can now, more than ever, be directed solely at the Web environment, allowing you to both design and build a website solely in Photoshop, or use the software to design unrivalled graphics for your online presence. But now, it's over to you...

```
                    <DT>Size: 17.94K</DT>
                    <DT>Settings: Quality is 60, Non-Progressive, Optimized on</DT></DL
            <PRE>
                        <CODE>
HTML>
HEAD>
TITLE> amazing1 PHO /TITLE>
META HTTP-EQUIV="Content-Type" CONTENT="text/html; charset=iso-8859-1">
/HEAD>
BODY BGCOLOR=#FFFFFF>
|-- ImageReady Slices (amazing1 PHO.jpg) -->
IMG SRC="amazing1-PHO.jpg" WIDTH=640 HEIGHT=480>
|-- End ImageReady Slices -->
/BODY>
/HTML> .</CODE></PRE></TD>
    </TR>
ABLE>
ODY>
HTML>
```

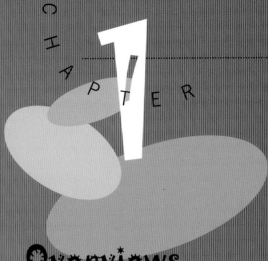

Overviews

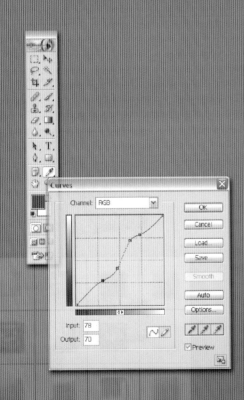

Adobe's Photoshop has, in the space of a few years, established itself as the premier image-editing and manipulation application among photographers and design professionals. Being both comprehensive and expandable gives it the ability to meet virtually every need—from simple color correction through to generating the color separations required for commercial printing.

¹⁰ THE PHOTOSHOP FAMILY

As a mass-market or general-purpose application Photoshop did not, in its early days, meet with the same level of success it enjoyed as a professional application. The extensive tool set was too detailed for the needs of the enthusiast, and the learning curve too steep.

Adobe went some way toward addressing this with the release of a "Limited Edition" version that retained the features crucial from a photographic standpoint, but which omitted high-end, prepress elements. And to meet the demands of consumer-level users, Adobe provided its Photodeluxe products. The Limited Edition (LE) version enjoyed modest success. Users had the power of the Photoshop engine, but were shielded from many of the functions that were irrelevant to them. But it was still, ostensibly, a professional product that lacked the "friendly face" of some rival applications.

The marketplace was also evolving. Website design, once the preserve of professional design houses, was now, by virtue of WYSIWYG (what-you-see-is-what-you-get) applications, something that anyone could at least attempt. It was no longer necessary to understand the programming language of the Web, HTML (see page 16). Anyone with even modest desktop publishing skills could feel instantly at home and create acceptable results. More significantly, the facilities to create webpages were now a fundamental part of the suite of tools in many emergent image-editing applications.

Adobe's response was as significant as it was low key. With the intermediate Version 5.5 of Photoshop came ImageReady, a sibling that offered much of Photoshop's core functionality (slanted toward the needs of Web designers) along with a raft of creative Web tools. ImageReady has continued to evolve and some of its Web-specific tools have made their debut in Photoshop itself.

Aimed at the growing needs of digital camera users, as well as what Adobe calls "serious enthusiast" photographers, Photoshop Elements joined the family. Offering the same fundamental tools as Photoshop (but again trimmed of its prepress features), Elements added useful image-repair and fixing tools. Hints and Recipes debuted

1 *Image editing is Photoshop's strength, but it offers much more, particularly for the website designer.*

2 *ImageReady's functions, such as Web optimization, have been created specifically with the website designer in mind.*

3 *Photoshop Elements, though lacking many of the Web-specific tools, is perfect for creating superior graphics and images, particularly if you've had little or no experience of the "full version" of Photoshop.*

too, offering solutions to common image-manipulation problems that now help newcomers through their early days of exploration. Today, Photoshop is a family, not a single product.

- **Photoshop** itself provides the tools to meet virtually all eventualities and, along with newly created Web features, is ideal for all Web-based image and graphics projects.
- **ImageReady** adds Web functionality—from animation creation through to Web optimization.
- **Photoshop Elements**, though lacking many Web-specific tools, is an ideal choice for creating superior graphics and images—particularly if you've had no prior experience of the Photoshop environment.

The majority of projects in this book are achievable with any variant of Photoshop. It is only when we come to some of the specific Web features (such as creating animations, image maps, and rollover states) that Photoshop 6 and upward or ImageReady 3 will be required. The illustrations, incidentally, are mainly from Photoshop 7.

Clipart

Clipart is variable in quality—and, sadly, much of it is poor. Good-quality material is rarely free and never unique. Creating your own images and graphics takes little effort and a few easily gained skills. However, you could use clipart in rough layouts, prior to incorporating your own artwork.

Photoshop as a Web tool

Should you use Photoshop as your main platform for creating Web imagery and graphics? Many argue that it's unnecessary, since Web designers are unlikely to use many of Photoshop's features. But in a world where graphics can be crucial to the efficacy of a website, having the best tools to create them is essential. Be mindful too that Photoshop provides a host of opportunities beyond Web graphics—photo retouching is the obvious example. Of course, even free website-building software can create an entire website for you, but it makes sense, when aiming for quality, to use the finest tools. That makes Photoshop a good choice when it comes to designing an interface that visitors will enjoy.

3

4

5

6

4|5|6 *Clipart varies in quality. While this image of a car is quite adequate, the boat image is well below par in technical terms. The carpenter graphic might be ideal for inclusion, but is likely to have been used before.*

12 PHOTOSHOP AND THE WEB

How can you exploit Photoshop's unique power? This book will show you how it can improve your photographs and images. Image manipulation is still the area in which Photoshop excels, but we'll also be looking at these features in the specific context of creating images and graphics for the Web. We'll look at how Photoshop can be used to make the devices—buttons, slices, animations, and rollovers—that contribute to the mechanics of a website. Additionally, the book will explain how you can create a unique interface for your website using the most basic tools. The overall aim is to use the minimum of effort to create something effective, meaningful—and useful.

The goal must be to create inspirational images to distinguish equally inspiring websites. In a world where new sites are being created literally by the second, we'll show you how to make your site stand out from the rest in quality and function.

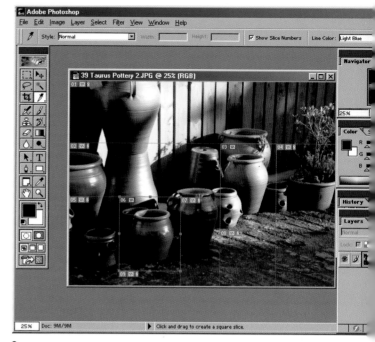

2

1 *Lack of time is no longer an excuse. This simple Web homepage was created in minutes and went "live" in under an hour. Over the page we'll illustrate how the graphic was produced.*

2 *The latest versions of Photoshop feature many webpage-creation tools, such as the Image Slicer, shown here.*

3 *ImageReady is capable of creating webpages and all the elements within them. Here mouse rollover states are being created "live".*

4 *Image optimizing is crucial when those images are being used for Web applications. ImageReady not only makes conventional optimization simple, but also enables advanced techniques such as selective optimization.*

3

1

The virtual universe

5 *Here's a screengrab from the Virtual Universe website. It was created entirely within Photoshop and includes many of the website interface elements that we'll be exploring through the course of this book.*

14   CREATING "OUR AMAZING WEBSITE"

Here's how to make this simple website homepage.
If you're not familiar with Photoshop or image
manipulation in general, don't worry if some of the
terms seem alien to you. We'll be looking more
closely at these later—and, of course, you can
always turn to the Glossary at the back of the book
for quick reference at any time.

   If you're reasonably fluent in Photoshop then
following these steps should take you 15 minutes,
or a half hour at most. If you've also got some
experience of designing and building webpages,
you'll notice that this project is very basic. What
about the size of our graphic? And the color palette?
Is it optimized? These questions—and many more
—will be addressed later.

⑤

⑥

⑦

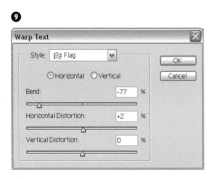

⑧

⑨

Warp Text

Style: Flag

OK
Cancel

○ Horizontal ○ Vertical

Bend: -77 %

Horizontal Distortion: +2 %

Vertical Distortion: 0 %

⑩

LET US TAKE YOU ON A MAGICAL TOUR OF DISCOVERY

❶ Use this sunset image for the background: it is bold but attractively simple. It isn't going to distract, or compete with, any text that is laid over the top of it. Open the image in Photoshop and create a duplicate layer. Use colors from the sunset and the *Gradient* tool to fill the background with a gentle gradient.

❷ Select the layer. Use the *Elliptical* and *Rectangular* marquees to select a curved area to the right. This will be where you'll place some buttons later on. Delete this area to let the background show through.

❸ Use the *Drop Shadow* command (*Layer > Layer Style > **Drop Shadow***) to give the layer a slight shadow, lifting it from the background.

❹ Next add a title, choosing a bold style and color.

❺ Add a drop shadow and an Inner Glow (*Layer Style*) to make the text stand out.

❻❼ Select the button areas using the *Rectangular Marquee* and use a style (dragged and dropped from the *Styles Palette*) to create a button.

❽ Because the buttons will be used to navigate the website, label them appropriately.

❾ For a final flourish, add a line of text introducing the site and use a *Flag Text Warp* to give it a curl.

❿ Additional navigational opportunities (to locations less likely to be used than those indicated by the buttons) have been indicated by text on the main picture.

16

HTML AND THE LANGUAGES OF THE WEB

There is an inherent contradiction in Web design. On the one hand, it is uniquely concerned with creating great visuals, but on the other there is this thing called HTML, a programming language that may need to be addressed.

HTML basics

HTML has the pivotal role in website creation because it is HTML that allows information on the Web to be displayed in a browser, which is your computer's interface with the Web. Thankfully, the nature and intended market for Web applications is such that users are often shielded from HTML. Only if or when changes occur that are beyond the capabilities of your application do you need to delve into this netherworld.

As programming languages go, HTML or HyperText Markup Language, is both simple and reasonably easy for anyone to follow. It also has the benefit of being written in "normal" characters —the "ASCII" text characters that are common to all major computer platforms. There are no compatibility issues, therefore an HTML document compiled on a Windows PC can be read and even edited on a Macintosh.

HTML, like any language, is in a constant state of evolution, and the shifting requirements of the Internet have dictated most of the changes. In most respects this is good. You can use new tools and features to take advantage of up-to-date browser technology and the increasing power of computers. But there's a downside too: only the most recent Web browsers will be able to understand and interpret the latest code. So creating a website that doesn't disenfranchise those people with earlier versions of browsers may involve some compromise.

So do you need to use, or even be familiar with, HTML? That's a hard question to answer definitively. There's no doubt that familiarity with HTML is a bonus, but equally there are website artists and photographers who have created

1 *This page from the* What Digital Camera *website is a typical index page providing links onward to supplementary pages, along with navigational tools.*

2 *The HTML code for the* What Digital Camera *website page shown opposite is simple, listing the images used and giving the links to the noted supplementary pages.*

3 *Here's what* Our Amazing Website *looks like viewed as HTML source code.*

3

```
<HTML>
<HEAD>
<TITLE>amazing1 PHO</TITLE>
<META HTTP-EQUIV="Content-Type" CONTENT="text/html; charset=
</HEAD>
<BODY BGCOLOR=#FFFFFF>
<!-- ImageReady Slices (amazing1 PHO.jpg) -->
<IMG SRC="amazing1-PHO.jpg" WIDTH=640 HEIGHT=480>
<!-- End ImageReady Slices -->
<TABLE WIDTH="80%" BORDER=1 CELLPADDING=1 CELLSPACING=2
        <TR>
              <TD>
                    <DL>
                    <DT>Format: JPEG</DT>
                    <DT>Dimensions: 640w x 480h</DT>
                    <DT>Size: 17.94K</DT>
                    <DT>Settings: Quality is 60, Non-Progres
                    <PRE>
                          <CODE>
&lt;HTML&gt;
&lt;HEAD&gt;
&lt;TITLE&gt;amazing1 PHO&lt;/TITLE&gt;
&lt;META HTTP-EQUIV="Content-Type" CONTENT="text/html; charset=i
&lt;/HEAD&gt;
&lt;BODY BGCOLOR=#FFFFFF&gt;
&lt;!-- ImageReady Slices (amazing1 PHO.jpg) --&gt;
&lt;IMG SRC="amazing1-PHO.jpg" WIDTH=640 HEIGHT=480&gt;
&lt;!-- End ImageReady Slices --&gt;
&lt;/BODY&gt;
&lt;/HTML&gt;</CODE></PRE></TD>
        </TR>
</TABLE>
</BODY>
</HTML>
```

```
2/
camera.com/0202/top.html
-digital-camera.com/0202/Resources/newtoppercopy.jpe
-digital-camera.com/0202/Resources/subs.gif
-digital-camera.com/0202/Resources/newtoppercopy1.jp
-digital-camera.com/0202/Resources/_clear.gif
-digital-camera.com/0202/Resources/_clear.gif
-digital-camera.com/0202/Resources/_clear.gif
-digital-camera.com/0202/Resources/_clear.gif
-digital-camera.com/0202/Resources/_clear.gif
-digital-camera.com/0202/Resources/_clear.gif
camera.com/0202/sidebar.html

p://www.what-digital-camera.com/0202/sidebar.html
:ation/x-www-form-urlencoded (default)

-digital-camera.com/0202/Resources/sideba1.gif
-digital-camera.com/0202/Resources/backis3.gif
-digital-camera.com/0202/Resources/wdc55cover.gif
```

marvelous work without ever writing a single part of it directly into HTML. We'll make the reasonable assumption in this book that you have no previous knowledge of it. Any HTML that is important (or even interesting) will be introduced along the way.

If you are now feeling curious about HTML there's an easy way to see how your work—or indeed anyone else's—is interpreted in HTML. Use your favorite browser to view your graphic. If you use Netscape, select *View menu* > **View Source**. In Internet Explorer use *View* > **Source**.

The masters of HTML

You can find out more about the latest HTML version by visiting the World Wide Web Consortium (usually referred to as W3C) at *www.w3.org*. W3C sets and monitors the standards of HTML and is the final arbiter of all proposed changes. So it is a good idea to bookmark this site and drop in occasionally. It is full of information and news that could be pertinent to your work—even if you are determined to ignore HTML entirely.

W3C WORLD WIDE WEB consortium

Leading the Web to its Full Potential...

Activities | Technical Reports | Site Index | About W3C | Cont

The World Wide Web Consortium (W3C) develops interoperable technologies (specifications, guidelines, softwar potential as a forum for information, commerce, communication, and collective understanding. On this page, you' information about W3C technologies and getting involved in W3C. We encourage you to learn more about W3C.

W3C A to Z

- Accessibility
- Amaya
- Annotea
- CC/PP
- CSS
- CSS Validator
- Device Independence
- DOM
- HTML
- HTML Tidy
- HTML Validator
- HTTP
- Internationalization
- Jigsaw
- Libwww
- MathML
- Micropayments
- Mobile
- Patent Policy
- PICS

▶ **VoiceXML 2.0 Promises Speech and Phone Services for the Web**

23 October 2001 : W3C is pleased to announce the first public Working Drai Voice Extensible Markup Language (VoiceXML) Version 2.0 and a Memorandu Understanding issued jointly with the VoiceXML Forum. VoiceXML uses XML bring synthesized speech, spoken and touch-tone input, digitized audio, recordir telephony, and computer-human conversations to the Web. Read the press relea testimonials, and visit the Voice Browser home page. (News archive)

▶ **XML Encryption Last Call Working Drafts Published**

18 October 2001 : The XML Encryption Working Group has released three I Call Working Drafts. XML Encryption Requirements provides XML syntax and processing requirements for encrypting digital content. XML Encryption Syntax Processing specifies a process for encrypting data and representing the result in EncryptedData element for cipher data. Decryption Transform for XML Signa enables the repeated encryption and signing of parts of XML documents. Comm are welcome through 9 November. Read about the W3C XML Encryption Activ (News archive)

18 Other Web design technologies

Apart from HTML you may, from time to time, come across other technologies in this area. Knowledge or understanding of these is not crucial to the subjects covered in this book, but the following terms are likely to arise as you begin to develop your site and study the work of others.

Dynamic HTML, or DHTML, is a form of HTML that accommodates more advanced features such as cascading style sheets (a feature concerned with the appearance of elements on a webpage) and JavaScript (see below), with the aim of allowing designers to create more dynamic webpages.

XML, which stands for Extensible Markup Language, enables users to create customized tags (the code that identifies an element, such as a heading, in an HTML document). This tends to be used more where complex databasing is required.

Flash, from Macromedia, is both a technology and the name of a product. It is used for animating vector graphics and can be used to display images and other media.

TIP

Websites and webpages

The Web has its own, precise vocabulary but, confusingly, terms are often used interchangeably and even erroneously. Here are the formal definitions of website and webpage, two terms that are notoriously swapped.

A **webpage** is a document on the World Wide Web that consists of an HTML file and associated graphics and image files. Most webpages will contain a link to another webpage.

A **website** is a group of HTML documents (with their respective graphics and image files). In effect, it is a collection of webpages interconnected with links, which permit navigation between each.

1 iHotelier® makes extensive use of Flash for its hotel room reservation service.

2 Compact, easy-to-download games are a favorite use of Shockwave.

3 This example of Java creates an x's and o's game to play against the computer.

2

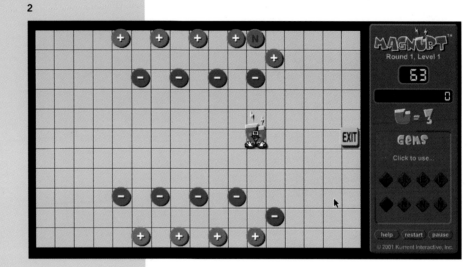

3

```
int pickRandom() {
    // randomly pick a number from 0 to 8 as the index of the chosen square
    boolean found = false;
    int pickedSquare = -1;
    do {
        pickedSquare = (int) (Math.random() * 9);   // 0 to 8
        if ( ! squares[pickedSquare].getLabel().equals("X") &&
           ! squares[pickedSquare].getLabel().equals("O") ) {
            // square not occupied
            found = true;
        }
    } while ( ! found );
    return pickedSquare;
} // end pickRandom()

void computerMove() {

    int pickedSquare;

    // try to make a win
    pickedSquare = makeWin();

    // if not successful, try make a block
    if ( pickedSquare == -1 )
        pickedSquare = makeBlock();

    // if not successful, just pick random
    if ( pickedSquare == -1 )
        pickedSquare = pickRandom();

    // mark the picked square as "O"
    squares[pickedSquare].setLabel("O");
    return;
}
```

Shockwave, also from Macromedia, is a technology that permits applications created in Macromedia's authoring application Director to be embedded in a webpage. Browsers require a Shockwave plug-in to display Shockwave material. This plug-in will also display Flash elements (but bear in mind that a Flash plug-in will only display Flash elements).

Java This is a high-level programming language that permits the creation of powerful applications that are platform independent. It is something you are unlikely to encounter with regard to the creation of Web graphics.

JavaScript With little connection to Java, JavaScript is a scripting language that can be used to create scripts for insertion into HTML. The browser will interpret the JavaScript seamlessly, just as if it were in HTML.

²⁰ WEB BROWSERS

The interface that allows us to connect to the Internet and webpages is called the Web browser (or just "browser"). There are many browser applications, which actually do much of the hard work of presenting a website. It is the browser, for example, that determines how a page is going to look. When you type in the address of a webpage and that page is downloaded to your computer, the browser reads the data and, after identifying the HTML commands, interprets the page in the way the creator intended. Or rather, as we shall see later, *largely* as the creator intended, as subtle differences between settings in alternative browser types can lead to different screen representations. Therefore, it is important to ensure that any graphics or images you create can be accurately reproduced on any mainstream browser and on any of the principal computer platforms.

Explorer vs. Navigator

For many computer users the term "browser" is synonymous with Microsoft's Internet Explorer, the browser that was infamously bundled with Windows 98, to the anger of Netscape and other makers of rival products. It is also the default browser for Macintosh computers, and a version of it was made available for the launch of Macintosh OS X.

Although Internet Explorer holds a lion's share of the browser market, there are others, including Netscape Navigator. This commands a significant (and loyal) following and in many technical respects is evenly matched with Internet Explorer. Netscape 6 is worthy of mention because it uses open-source codings (source code that is available to anyone to develop). Unlike many applications that tend to add dozens of new features with each new version, Netscape 6 was designed to be compact and weighs in at around 10MB (compared with the 17MB of Internet Explorer 6).

In a world in which two browsers seem to be in a fight to the death, any attempt to introduce more would seem futile. Against the odds, however, Opera, a browser from a Norwegian Company of the same name, has confounded the online pundits and developed a healthy following. Much

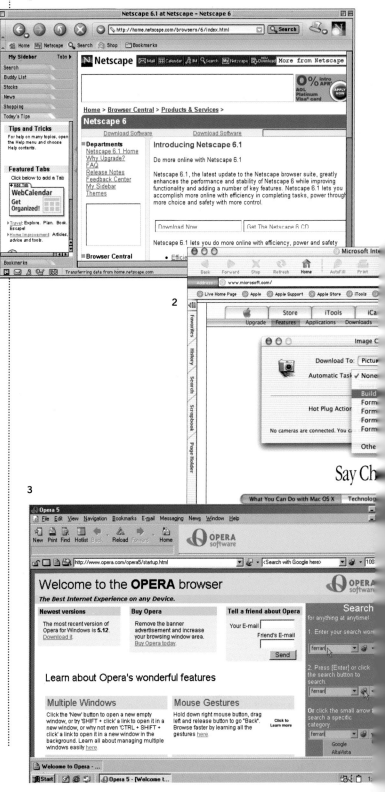

1 *With interchangeable interface elements (Skins) the look of Netscape 6 can be customized to the user's preferences. Additional features and links can also be included in the sidebar.*

2 *Internet Explorer is widely available and is the default choice for many computers. The launch of Mac OS X saw a special version that was supplied for this operating system (pictured). For the PC, version 6 of Internet Explorer differs little from version 5 visually, but has enhanced security features. It also features a novel way of displaying large images, which can be scaled to fit the screen.*

3 *Opera's boasts of speed and security have won it many converts, making it a browser that should be taken very seriously.*

4 ITV Active *is typical of set-top box Internet services that offer comprehensive facilities, but are limited with respect to graphics. Note the use of TV-remote teletext color buttons for navigation shortcuts.*

4

of Opera's success has stemmed from its claim to be the "fastest browser on Earth." This is true in many respects, and a lot of users who have turned to Opera also say that it is simpler to use and more secure. With few of the embellishments that more established browsers add with each update, Opera can concentrate on the basic task of downloading and interpreting webpages. Like other browsers it is available for Windows (95 and onwards, and XP) and Macintosh (8.5 onward and OS X).

Browser blues

If you have already spent time surfing you've probably come across sites that just don't seem to work. Whether it's a link that isn't active or text that is drawn across a crucial image you are likely to put it down to an HTML error, a computer glitch, or bug. You might be correct in that assumption, but chances are the site's creator has committed the cardinal cyber-sin of not testing his or her site with every Web browser on every platform.

The Web on TV

There's a family of browsers that we've not discussed so far. These are the Internet-through-your-TV and interactive TV-based browsers whose names you might not be familiar with, such as iTV Active and WebTV.

If you ever have call to create material specifically for these browsers then different sets of rules apply. A lack of memory restricts the quality of graphics within them, while the absence of a mouse (in most) dictates that conventional remote control keys are used for navigation. You'll also have to use more muted colors than you can on a computer monitor. This is because TV screens are designed with higher contrast to the point that conventional Web graphics would be too bright. Although such browsers are beyond our scope here, you can expect them and their set-top boxes to grow in both power and number in the future.

22 PHOTOS, GRAPHICS, AND TEXT ON THE WEB

Introducing Web file formats

If you work in desktop-publishing applications you'll probably be familiar with a range of image and graphics formats. Other than those native to specific applications (for example Photoshop's own .psd format) you'll probably have worked with .tiff and Encapsulated PostScript (.eps) files. Due to their large file size, these are great for achieving the maximum quality on the printed page. For Web use, however, the needs are different and are dictated by the bandwidth of Internet connections. Bandwidth determines how much and how fast data can be downloaded to a computer and is a crucial consideration in many Web-graphic applications. The fastest conventional modems can manage less than 7KB per second (and often much less than this), which precludes the use of multimegabyte images or graphics for webpages. Therefore, for Web use, you need to be familiar with some different file types: JPEG, GIF, and PNG.

JPEG – Joint Photographic Experts Group

Those who use, or are familiar with, digital cameras will recognize the JPEG format since it is often used for image storage in such cameras. This is because of its ability to compress files to one percent (in extreme cases) of their original size. This makes it ideal for the Web too. A good-sized image can be compressed for transmission and then restored on arrival at the recipient's computer. And because the file size is small, the image will download much more quickly.

The payback for this compression is that the process is "lossy." This means that it is only achieved by discarding a substantial amount of data, which can never be restored. JPEG images have—to a greater or lesser degree—a characteristic "blocked" appearance. The more an image is compressed, the more "blocked" it will be. And the effect is cumulative: if a JPEG image is opened and saved a number of times, especially at maximum compression, the degradation in quality becomes

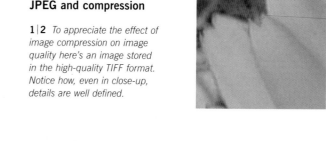

JPEG and compression

1|2 *To appreciate the effect of image compression on image quality here's an image stored in the high-quality TIFF format. Notice how, even in close-up, details are well defined.*

3|4 *The same image has now been saved as a JPEG file and has had a hefty amount of compression applied to it. The full image, at the small scale reproduced here, does not look very different. Study the close-up section and the loss of definition and blocking becomes obvious.*

5 *When the image has been opened and saved a number of times (as it might be when editing the image over several sessions) the cumulative effect of the compression is clear.*

GIF

6|7 *The GIF format permits a maximum of 256 colors. The original full-color image here is shown as both a TIF (with 16.7 million colors) and a GIF with 256 colors. Even allowing for the limitations in printing, there is little discernible difference between the two at this size.*

8 *Reducing the number of colors to 64 reduces the file size by a factor of 10. The reduction causes obvious blocking and posterization in some areas of the image but is otherwise an acceptable representation.*

9|10 *Reducing the number of colors further (to 16 and 8 respectively) further compresses the file size but now the effects of a limited color palette are more obvious. For some uses (for example small image thumbnails) this might still be acceptable, but for more exacting uses, too much quality has been sacrificed.*

The PNG advantage

11|12 *The PNG format may be the Cinderella of image and graphics formats but, since it has some of the best features of JPEG and GIF, it deserves more widespread acceptance. Here, for example, a PNG graphic (the text) can feature transparency to enable a drop shadow. Furthermore, the same graphic can contain 16.7 million colors, which enables it to reproduce images effectively.*

very noticeable. To use it successfully you need to balance the degree of compression with acceptable download times. The compression blocking also makes the format unsuitable for graphics and text.

GIF – Graphical Interchange Format

Although the GIF file format can only achieve modest compression (around 4:1), there is no loss of quality (which is why it is known as lossless). The GIF format (originally introduced by CompuServe—now part of AOL—for the distribution of graphics over the Web) allows a more limited color palette than JPEG (256 colors instead of 16.7 million) and is therefore better suited to graphics or image thumbnails (where full color rendition is less important). GIFs also support Transparency and Animation.

The use of Transparent GIFs enables non-rectangular images to be placed on a webpage and allows the text to flow around the edges of the image in much the same way as text can be wrapped around a graphic in desktop publishing. Animated GIFs use the rapid switching of image layers to create the impression of conventional animation. The results are surprisingly effective and they don't require the large file sizes of traditional animations.

PNG – Portable Network Graphics Format

The PNG format offers modest (around 30 percent lossless) compression along with support for 16 million colors and transparency but does not support animation. As a compromise between GIF and JPEG formats it succeeds, but has not been fully accepted by all the principal Web browsers (some of which require a special plug-in to use PNG files). But the level of acceptance is rising.

6

7

8

9

10

11

12

24 Bitmaps and vectors

Digital photographs are built from pixels, the smallest of picture elements. This makes them resolution dependent. In other words, as you enlarge a pixel-based image, you'll soon reach a point where the pixels become visible. As the enlargement continues these pixels merely enlarge and no further detail becomes visible: the image becomes, as designers say, "pixelated."

Some graphics applications, notably Adobe's Illustrator and Macromedia's Freehand, are vector-based. When you construct illustrations in these applications the shapes are defined mathematically as vectors. Each element—color fills and points, as well as shape outlines—are determined as part of a mathematical expression for the illustration. When you enlarge (or reduce) the size of a vector illustration you change the scale mathematically so that the image is redrawn at the new size. Therefore, all the detail is retained, no matter what size the image is scaled to.

Photoshop is still, ostensibly, a bitmap application but it does feature a range of vector-based tools that you can use to create vector graphics and add them to other images.

1|2 *Enlarge any part of a bitmap image and the pixels become visible.*

3 *Vector illustrations are independent of the resolution at which they are created, viewed or printed, and can therefore be redrawn at any scale.*

3

Drawing or painting?

As well as the precise bitmap and vector, certain other terms are used to distinguish between the graphics types: "Drawing" and "Painting" are often used, for example. In computing terms, Painting describes the action of coloring or tinting pixels with a painting tool. Once pixels are painted there is no way to move the brushstroke to another position (apart from using the Undo command and repeating the paint action).

Drawing involves creating vector shapes that can, where required, be individually selected and moved to a new location. These shapes are often referred to as object-oriented. It is easy to select, move, resize, and even change the outline (known as the path) of a shape. Similarly the line thicknesses that describe the shape and fill color (known as attributes) can be changed at will.

The Photoshop pen

The Pen tool (which, for those not familiar with it, is not a painting tool) has long been a feature of Photoshop. It is used for creating paths (i.e. vector shape outlines), which can, usefully, be applied to the bitmapped image to create selections.

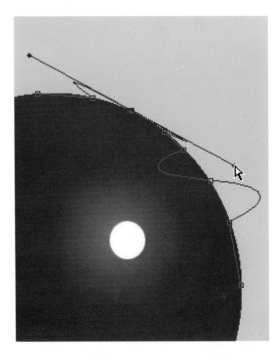

26   Text and type

Although you should approach applying text directly to images with caution, for the purposes of the Web and other graphic (rather than photographic) applications, text is essential.
It would be fair to say that Adobe itself considered text to be of secondary importance for a long time. In earlier versions, the text options offered in Photoshop were deemed sufficient, but still lagged behind page layout and wordprocessing programs in terms of their comprehensiveness. This neglect has been put right. In more recent versions the text options have become increasingly sophisticated, with Photoshop 7, for example, providing a long-overdue spell checker!

When you add text to an image in Photoshop it is created in a new Type Layer automatically. Placing it in a layer gives you obvious flexibility. You can edit the text and, if appropriate, move it relative to the underlying image.

❶ Before entering your text, click on the *Text* button in the toolbar. You can then choose a font and text size. Also, select a text color (by clicking on the swatch shown in the *Tool Options* palette).

❷ Enter your text. You can enter as much or as little as you require, using the *Character* and *Paragraph* palettes for additional levels of control.

❸ To position or adjust the position of the text, click on the *Move* tool, ensuring that the *Type Layer* is still the selected layer.

❹ If you have made any mistakes in your spelling or formatting you can reselect the type tool and make appropriate changes there.

❺ You can set multiple type layers in your image. Each type layer can then be moved in relation to the others or (using the *Layers* palette features) grouped and moved relative to the remaining layers. To create a new type layer, click on the *Type* tool and then place the I-beam cursor at the point you wish the new text to begin.

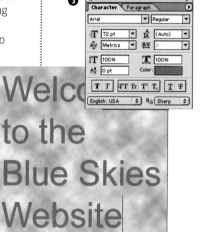

❻ Using the layer style *Stroke* gives the edges of the text characters greater definition. It enables you to use colors very close to the background color to be used if required.

❼ Drop shadow is another useful way of lifting text from a background. The shadow does tend to create additional colors. If your are working with a limited color palette, this could be an issue.

❽ Similarly, edge glows have a useful separating effect.

❾ ❿ Avoid some color combinations, such as colors are that are too similar or too contrasting. They will either discourage visitors, or simply be very discourage to read.

❻

❼

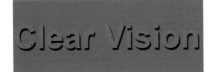

❽

❾

❿

11 *Photoshop permits several levels of antialiasing, from None (left) through to Smooth (right).*

Clear Vision

When using text on an image you are not constrained within the same limited range of fonts that can be successfully used in HTML. You can use any font, and each will ultimately become an indelible part of the image. You should, however, remain mindful of clarity when placing text over an image. It is important that your text is easily read by a site visitor and that colors do not clash or make the text difficult to read.

We can use several "dodges" (explored in more detail later) to solve potential color clashes or improve clarity.

Antialiasing

Antialiasing is an optional enhancement to text, producing type that is smoothed at the edges. This is achieved by partially filling the edge pixels with a blend of the type and background colors. This makes the type easier to read but has some drawbacks when used on the Web because a large number of colors are introduced in the smoothing process. This compromises your ability to reduce the colors in an image when optimizing the file size. Fortunately, there are ways of avoiding this problem and maintaining legibility, which we will investigate later on.

Rasterizing type layers

The nature of some filter effects and painting tools is such that they cannot work with type layers. If your image features type layers then you'll be prompted to rasterize the type first. This process (also achieved by using the Rasterize command) renders the type layer as a conventional bitmap, so subsequent type editing becomes impossible.

11

28   Dithering and the missing colors

One of the ways in which file sizes can be kept to a minimum when sent to browsers is by restricting the number of colors in an image. For some graphics this is not a problem—many graphics can be accurately reproduced with only a handful of colors. But if you were to restrict the number of colors in an image to, say, 256 how would this affect the way it looks in the browser?

There is the strong possibility that the image will look "posterized", which means that it will have been broken down into blocks of color that represent the nearest equivalent to that 256.

To counteract this possibility—at least to a degree—browsers employ the process of dithering. Where a color is outside the range available, the browser attempts to simulate the color from a mix of those that are available. It's a process rather like that used by inkjet printers (and, indeed, by commercial printers) where full color images are created from only three colored inks plus black.

Pattern or diffusion?

Two dithering techniques are used for color representation in browsers; pattern dithering and diffusion dithering. Pattern dithering is considered the less satisfactory option: intermediate colors are produced by using a regular pattern of pixels. This can produce unpleasant coloration and patterning on large expanses of color (where dithering is often required) that seriously degrade image quality. Diffusion dithering achieves its color simulation by using an apparently more random pattern of pixels.

The original gradient (left) is shown here in ImageReady with no dither (second from left), diffusion dither (second from right), and pattern dither (right).

The posterized effect is okay for an image thumbnail but is unacceptable for a quality image.

Color is one of the problematic areas of Web graphics. In the more familiar world of desktop publishing, variables are pretty much kept to a minimum and are, largely, under our control. On the Web, however, matters are more contentious. You must be mindful that many of those who view your work will have monitors that display a full range of 16.7 million colors but others might

Original: "Untitled-1.tif...
410K

GIF
4.577K
3 sec @ 28.8Kbps

display just 256. Those monitors may or, more probably, may not be set correctly. Browser choice —something else that is entirely out of your hands—will vary from user to user. And each browser may have different display parameters too.

You could settle for the worst-case scenario and use limited palettes of color—the Web-safe palette —and live with the compromises this introduces, but few creative people are willing to do so. A common working practice is to use more comprehensive color palettes (such as adaptive or selective palettes) and test the resultant images against different browsers and computer platforms set to display 256 colors. You can then make the presumption that if the image looks good (or at least acceptable) under these circumstances, then they will look a lot better when a greater number of colors have been used.

.47K
sec @ 28.8Kbps

GIF
54.5K
20 sec @ 28.8Kbps

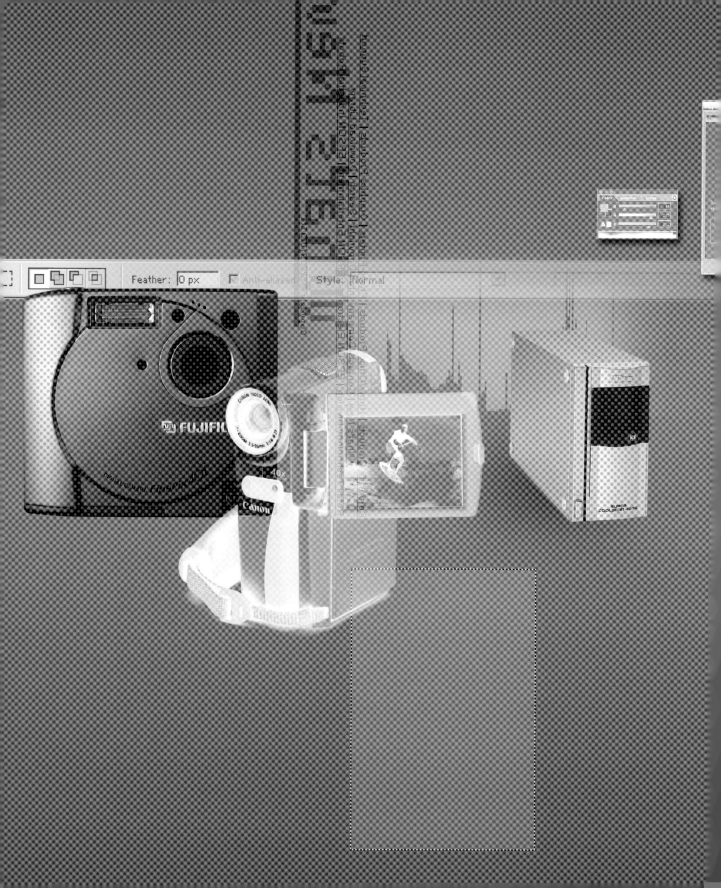

Feather: 0 px   ☐ Anti-aliased   Style: Normal

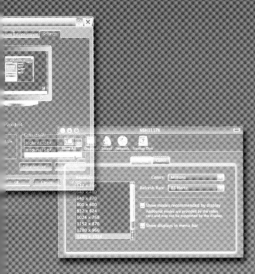

2

Getting Started

Creating successful digital artwork depends on many factors. Some of the necessary skills can be acquired through practice. Others, however, are more to do with good preparation and reading up on your hardware and software. Of course, it does not help that some instruction manuals can sometimes be dull, difficult to understand, or off-putting, so over the next few pages you'll find the essential, practical guide to getting started with Photoshop. We'll look at the methods by which you can acquire good images—and get the best results from your hardware and software investments. The key elements that contribute to good website practice are also described.

IMAGE ACQUISITION

Whether your aim is to source images for use on the Web, in print, or perhaps in business presentations, your goal should always be the same: to aim for the highest-quality results. Unfortunately, there is a strong belief, fostered by purveyors of mediocre media resources, that almost anything will do on the Web and that poor-quality material can, with a little postproduction, be made to work. Don't believe a word of it. That oft-used phrase "garbage in: garbage out" is as true for Web images as for any others.

It might be stating the obvious, but the prerequisite for Web images is that they should be in digital form. So let's look first at the varying means of getting your images into digital form and onto your computer.

There have never been so many options for doing this as there are today. So, whether your background is in photography and you have conventional or digital photographic equipment, or you have no photographic skills at all but still want to get good-quality images onto your website, one of these options will be right for you.

1

3

1 *A Nikon AF Nikkon 28:80mm lens, one of the interchangeable, high-quality lenses that are available even for many mid-market cameras.*

2 *An SLR (single-lens reflex) camera, which includes a variety of aperture and shutter speed presets. This one has a standard 35:70mm lens, but again it is interchangeable.*

3 *One of the many fully-automatic, autofocus "point and shoot" cameras flooding the market. This one has a motorized zoom and an integrated flash*

4 *A Nikon Pronea APS (Advanced Photography System) camera, which mixes "point and shoot" technology with some of the advantages of a 35mm SLR and a digital camera. APS film, though, is smaller format (28mm) and requires special developing.*

Conventional Cameras

Although the gap is narrowing between conventional cameras and their digital counterparts, the quality offered by conventional models—those that use traditional film—still gives them the edge. There is also an astonishing range of models available, from pocket-sized compacts through to comprehensively specified 35mm cameras, and the more substantial medium- and large-format models.

For most practical purposes 35mm cameras are ideal. Single-lens reflex (SLR) models, with their interchangeable lenses, are particularly useful. The wide range of controls and accessories they offer makes them suitable for most photographic needs and opportunities.

For digital purposes, the most obvious drawback of conventional cameras is their use of film as a recording medium. The result is that your photos will need to be digitized before you can use them on a computer. We'll look at some methods for doing this over the following pages.

There is also the question of immediacy: it takes time to get a film digitized, and you'll need to have your film processed first. This is a drawback for those users who need to "grab" a shot and put it on the website with minimal delay.

But where conventional cameras come into their own—even in the light of the continual advances made by digital cameras—is in quality. Even modest conventional models can provide excellent results, although you could argue that these are more than Web use requires.

34 Digital Cameras

Digital cameras have, in a very short period of time, come to rival conventional 35mm cameras in many aspects of their performance. The sheer variety of different models competing for your attention makes them difficult to classify by type, so the most meaningful classification for our purposes is in terms of their resolution.

Most digital cameras use Charge Coupled Device (CCD) sensors in place of film for recording a scene. These are small, electronic devices that comprise a compact grid of sensors (known as photosites). These are given an electrical charge prior to exposure to render them sensitive to light. The number of photosites essentially (but not exclusively) defines the resolution of the camera.

Photosites are also—confusingly, for computer users—generally described as pixels. A typical resolution might be from around 300,000 pixels (for an image of 640 x 480 pixels, in the other sense of the word) to 5 megapixels (5,000,000 pixels) for a good-quality SLR-type camera, and 18 megapixels or more for top-of-the-range models.

Images are either stored in the camera's onboard memory (in the case of cheaper models) or on removable memory cards. These come in a range of types. With the biggest share of the market, CompactFlash cards are used by cameras ranging from simple consumer devices to professional-level models. With the largest capacity measured in hundreds of megabytes (most manufacturers having gigabyte versions in their portfolio), CompactFlash is ideally suited to the multimegapixel camera. Images can be stored on them without compression.

T I P

Size matters

Both CCD and CMOS chips offer a smaller imaging area than the frame of a 35mm camera. A consequence is that lenses designed for both digital and conventional cameras tend to have a telephoto effect when used with the digital model.

1|2|3 *Unhindered by the limitations of film and film cartridges, digital cameras come in many and varied shapes, as these models from Fuji and Nikon illustrate.*

4 *Digital video cameras such as this model from Canon are able to record still images onto their memory cards*

SmartMedia cards are used by many inexpensive to midmarket cameras, and are nominally limited to a maximum capacity of 256 megabytes. Their ultracompact size precludes larger capacities, and they also lack the controller module (common to CompactFlash and some other formats) that is used to accelerate the downloading of an image from the camera to the card. Such controllers also make possible the rapid shooting of muiltiple images.

Other card formats include the Secure Digital (SD) MultiMediaCard, and the Memory Stick. Because each of these has effectively been "sponsored" by a manufacturer or group of manufacturers, they do not share the widespread market acceptance of SmartMedia or CompactFlash. Memory Stick, for example, is used exclusively in Sony equipment, where it has become a high-capacity replacement for the floppy disk. Sony digital video cameras, MP3 players, and personal digital assistants (PDAs) all use Memory Sticks.

But unless your memory format can be slotted directly into other devices, images are more usually downloaded from a digital camera using an appropriate cable (usually USB) and corresponding driver software. If the camera uses nonproprietary memory cards, an alternative, faster method is to use a card reader. These are small accessory boxes into which memory cards can be slotted, and which connect to a computer's USB socket. Some models are designed to accommodate only cards of a specific type, but others feature slots for two or more different formats. PC card versions are available for use with laptop computers.

4

Digital Video Cameras

Although the still image quality from analog video cameras is generally poor, stills from digital video (DV) models are at least worthy of consideration. Many of the top DV cameras feature Still Image or Snapshot modes that take "true" still images (rather than recording a frozen image to tape for a few seconds). This has become possible thanks to the inclusion of memory card slots in many models.

The quality of a still image from DV cameras when the Pause button is pressed during playback remains poor, even if it is theoretically better than the 640 x 480 pixels of a basic digital camera. However, in Snapshot mode a true still can, with the best equipment, have a resolution as high as 1.8 megapixels. Images of this original quality will be more than sufficient for many uses, including most Web applications.

Although a digital video camera is not as convenient as an equivalent still model, the Snapshot image mode could be useful if you need to gather both still and video footage simultaneously —from the same source—for use on the Web. Once an image or series of images has been recorded, it can be downloaded by the same basic process as for digital still cameras: direct from the camera, or via a card reader.

A word about CMOS sensors

CMOS—complementary metal oxide semiconductor —sensors are increasingly appearing as an alternative imaging chip to the CCD. CMOS chips tend to be cheaper to produce because they are based on the same technology used for manufacturing computer chips. Lower sensitivity has, however, precluded their use in all but the lower end of the digital camera market.

36 Stock Photography

So far we've made the assumption that you intend to take your own photographs. If you have neither the need nor the inclination to do this, there is a vibrant market for stock photographs that you can use to enliven your website at relatively low cost.

Much of this material is freely available—in the form of clipart collections or royalty-free CDs— but better-quality material tends to require payment each time it is used. The cost will vary both according to the supplier and to your intended use of the material. Use on a specialized website with comparatively few visitors will mean a smaller payment than if the image is intended for commercial, mass-market advertising purposes. Alternatively, some libraries offer unrestricted use for a flat-fee payment.

Try taking a look at the websites of Photodisc (*www.photodisc.com*) and of CreativePro.com to get an idea of the breadth of available material and of the cost involved. Stock images will be supplied in digital form as an Internet download or on a CD, but many libraries offer free use of low-resolution copies so that you can create rough layouts.

The term "stock" photography normally applies to "generic" material, such as pictures of office buildings that can be used in a wide range of applications. Most stock photography libraries will contain some more identifiable material, but it tends to be populist in nature—photos of tourist locations, for example. They will also carry "mood" pictures of families, children, business executives, and the like.

If you need a specific picture, such as a precise botanical specimen, or a particular building in a town off the main tourist routes, you'll need to delve a little deeper into the specialized websites. You can track these down either by using your favorite search engine or by visiting a website appropriate to the subject matter and following the relevant links. For geographical features, town and city (or regional) websites are an ideal place to start. Learned societies are another good resource. For example, the National Geographical Society in the US and Royal Geographic Society in the UK have very comprehensive geographic and ethnographic image libraries, plus links to many more.

1 *There are many online sources of stock photography. CreativePro offers single images and CD collections.*

2 *Photodisc's extensive catalog allows you to search both for specific images and more generally using keywords.*

3 *PhotoCD offers five image resolutions. The intermediate "base" resolution is designed to be viewed at the 72 pixels per inch of a computer monitor. (In terms of scanning and image resolution, pixels per inch, or ppi, and dots per inch, or dpi, are interchangeable.)*

1

2

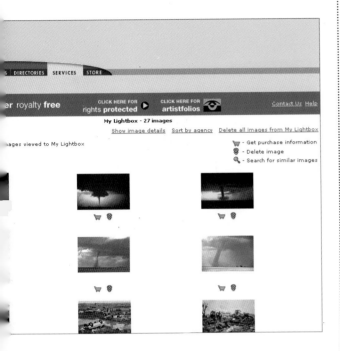

Photos on CD

We've discussed the delivery of stock images on CD, but nowadays CD can also be the delivery and storage medium of choice for your own pictures, in PhotoCD or PictureCD formats. Both can be produced by commercial photo-processors and in many ways are an ideal method of getting digital versions of your conventional photos.

Kodak developed PhotoCD in the early 1990s as a cross-platform method of scanning and storing photographs onto CD-ROM to support the emerging digital-imaging business. PhotoCDs can contain up to 100 images stored at five different resolutions from thumbnail through to large format (producing an 18MB file size from a 35mm original). Variants cater for even larger file sizes and the scanning of film media larger than 35mm. Scans tend to be good quality, but the process is expensive and tends to be regarded as a professional service, which means that the number of outlets now offering the service are limited.

More widely available is the PictureCD format that uses a basic method to store medium-sized (6MB from 35mm) files using the JPEG format. PictureCDs (a Kodak proprietary name) and equivalents from other companies also include basic image-editing and cataloging software designed to appeal to the consumer market. The quality offered by PictureCDs is quite sufficient for most purposes, including Web design.

3

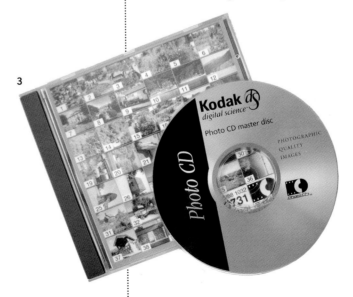

38 The Internet

There is no better place to find images on specialist subjects than the Internet. You'll quickly discover that you can surf an enormous number of resources, many of which are long-established, commercial or academic, and discover a whole world of resources that you probably never imagined was out there. Some of the major search engines, such as Google (*www.google.com*) also include an excellent and swift image-search facility.

The great thing about using the Web as a source for your material is that you can view it immediately on screen and at the resolution you are likely to use in your Web application. In most cases you can then download the image (having paid for it online, if appropriate) and begin work right away.

Scanners

The scanner provides the most successful and comprehensive way of digitizing media. Prints, flat artwork, transparent media and more can be quickly turned into digital files using a scanner.

The most common scanner is the Flatbed type, sometimes called the desktop scanner. These can be used to scan all opaque media—prints and flat artwork—and many models will also allow the scanning of transparent material, including transparencies and negatives.

TIP

The Numbers Game

If you are in the market for a new flatbed scanner then don't be seduced by comparatively inexpensive models that offer interpolated resolutions of 9,600 dpi or more. Interpolated resolutions are created by the scanner software, which introduces intermediate points based on the colour and lightness values of their neighbors. The result is an image file of substantial size that does not offer any more true detail than that of an optical resolution of, say, 1,200 dpi. If you need to interpolate an image you can achieve a better result later in Photoshop. You should concentrate on the optical resolution figure at this point.

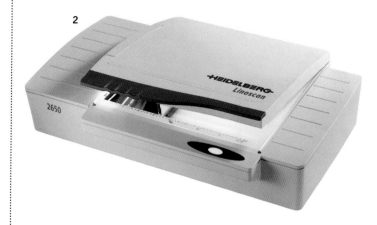

1 *Slide scanners such as this model from Nikon are capable of high resolution scans of medium format (and smaller) media and can, by virtue of included software, also remove dust and scratch marks along with other blemishes at the time of the scan.*

2 *High-resolution scanners such as this model from Heidelberg are able to make commendably good scans of transparent media.*

3 *This scanner from UMAX is a typical example of the good quality of consumer devices available today.*

4 *A flatbed scanner in miniature; a slide scanner can scan the precise frame area of the transparency.*

3

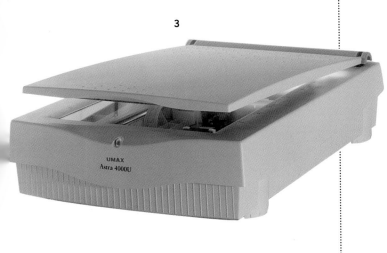

4

Flatbed models look like compact photocopiers, featuring a glass plate normally of Letter (or "A4") size upon which the original artwork is placed. A scan head, comprising a CCD array, passes underneath the plate and records the subject. The resolution at which the subject is scanned can be set in the scanner software, and optical resolutions of up to 2,400 lines per inch (lpi) are possible with top-end machines. The term optical resolution is used to make a distinction from interpolated resolution, a flawed method of creating high-resolution files from lower resolution scans. Because this does not increase the effective resolution from that of the original scan, it is of little consequence. When shopping for a scanner you should base your judgement on the optical resolution.

For larger originals, scanners are widely available in sizes of 11¾ x 16½ inches. The smaller market for these means that prices are often more than double those of equivalent legal/letter model. Many models also come with tranparency adaptors, sometimes called transparency hoods. These disengage the lighting source within the scanner and replace it with a source that illuminates transparent media from behind. It is thus possible to scan filmstock and other transparent material in the same way as you would a print. The drawback with scanning negatives and transparencies in this way has been the poor resolution of scanners with respect to the dimensions of (say) 35mm film frames. Contemporary scanners are capable of quite adequate scans and are often sufficient for Web applications. Where greater resolution is required however, a dedicated film scanner is necessary.

Film scanners work on the same fundamental principal as the flatbed scanner, but are designed to scan at very high resolution over the frame area of a film. Many models accept 35mm filmstock and also (usually via an adaptor) APS films, and are economically priced. Models for film as large as 5 x 4 inches are available—but they are not cheap.

If you have a few large transparencies it is often much more cost effective to have them scanned by a bureau specializing in such media.

Unlikely to be relevant to Web usage, even higher resolutions are possible using sophisticated drum scanners, but these tend to be used in high-quality magazine and book publication.

40 SUCCESSFUL SCANNING

Scanning a photograph on a flatbed scanner is theoretically an automatic process. But to ensure that every nuance of the original print is captured as faithfully as possible requires practice. Once you've gained an understanding of the processes involved, you'll be able to rescue your inferior or damaged prints as well.

Scanning software

All scanners come with scanning software designed to make scanning both simple and effective. The application shown here, VistaScan, (supplied with some UMAX scanners and typical of most scanning applications) features alternative interfaces for beginners and advanced users. In either mode, the first step is to make a preview scan, or prescan. During this fast, low-resolution scan the software will determine the focus and exposure settings required for the final scan. See the boxed text to learn about how to proceed in either beginner or advanced mode.

Beginner mode

In Vistascan, these steps are simple. Apply a crop to the preview (if an area smaller than the full-size plate is required).

Next, choose a scan type. The options are photograph, printed matter, text, and a Web-originated image. The type you select will determine the optimum resolution and any filtering that might be required. Scanning text for optical character recognition, for example, requires a relatively high resolution to achieve good results; photos from all printed matter will need a descreening filter to prevent image artifacts due to the printed dot pattern on the original artwork.

Selecting a scan type (in this software) automatically starts the full scan.

Advanced mode

In Advanced mode most of the settings have to be made manually. First you need to select a color mode. The options here include several colour and black-and-white options. Note the Web color option. While it is tempting (and faster) to scan using the more limited color range available on the Web, it is best to scan in full RGB color since you risk compromising any image manipulations by using Web colors at this stage.

Next, you should select the resolution. Web graphics will always be *viewed* at a nominal resolution of 72dpi, but note that at this point we are talking about the *scanning* resolution. If you scan a small image at 72dpi, but later decide to blow the scan up and display it larger on your website, the image quality will be compromised. It's always a good idea to scan at a higher resolution (say 300 or even 600dpi) and scale downward later.

Depending on the nature of the original, you can set a Descreen filter. This will remove artifacts due to interference between the scanner and the printing dots of the original, if it's taken from a magazine or other printed article. Scans of photos don't need descreening, but most printed matter will require some. Here you can set the scan to compensate for dots of different spacing, typical of newspaper (the coarsest), magazines, and fine art reproductions (the finest).

Additional filters may also be used while scanning to sharpen or soften the scanned image. Photoshop has all the tools to

1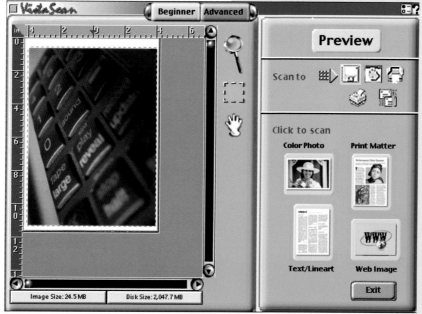

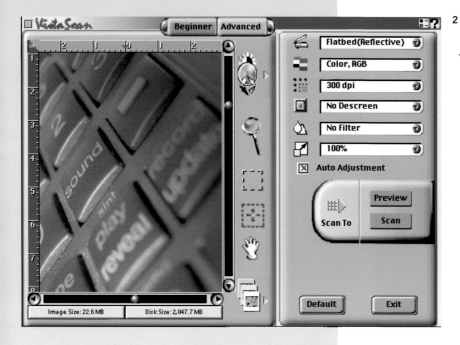

achieve similar results, so it is best to set this to No Filter.

Now hit the Scan button to perform the task. Note that some scanning software includes additional features to, for example, alter the color balance of a scan or even alter tonal and contrast ranges. We shall look at these ideas later as they appear in Photoshop, it is often useful to make some corrections to color or contrast at the time of scanning. Most other changes are not advised before importing your image into Photoshop.

3

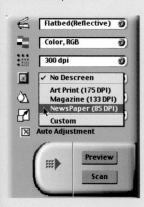

1 The Beginner modes of Uma 's VistaScan.

2 The Advanced modes of Umax's VistaScan.

2 RGB Colour is the best setting for our scan.

4 Descreen allows you to compensate for the screens used in the printing process of a variety of different media.

Scanning software is as important a factor in achieving a good scan as the hardware. Specialist scanning software includes products such as Binuscan's Color Pro Suite, which is interesting in that it makes the assumption that no original image is ever perfect and will try automatically to improve the image on scanning. Many scanning experts will decry this method on the basis that automatic corrections make too many presumptions about the image. However, the corrections are usually very effective, and the approach is ideal for those who have neither the time nor the experience to make adjustments themselves.

Other names to look out for include LinoColor (exclusive to Heidelberg scanners), which is probably the most comprehensive and effective, and Silverfast from LaserSoft Software.

You'll see in the examples on this page that we recommend scanning at a moderately high resolution of 300dpi (or ppi), or even 600dpi. But why should we do this when the screen resolution for Web images is the more pedestrian 72dpi and we will (in most cases) be rescaling the scanned imaged downward from the scanned size?

The simple answer is quality. Scanning at a high resolution gives us more leeway later to trim and resize the image. If we were to start with a 72dpi image, quality would be compromised as soon as we tried to resize.

42

Intended use	Image Size (inches)	Resolution (d/ppi)	RGB file size
Website thumbnail	1.5 x 1	90	32KB
Website full screen	9 x 7	90	1.45MB
6 x 4 inch print	6 x 4	300	6.5MB
Letter size print	12 x 8	300	27MB

Scanning resolutions

This table indicates the advised scanning resolutions for the required outputs and the file sizes generated.

When you first view your scanned image you might be disappointed. The image can appear "flat" (lacking in contrast) and—more significantly—will show some degree of dust and scratch invasion. No matter how fastidious you might be about keeping your scanner and artwork clean, you can expect some ingress. Fortunately, most scanning software now features routines that are designed to identify and eliminate marks judged to be alien during the scan.

Digital ICE[3] ("Ice Cubed") is a suite of three software packages by Applied Science Fiction Inc for the digital cleaning of images during scanning, and it is now standard on Nikon slide scanners (dust is a more significant problem for slides).

There is no set procedure for postprocessing a scan, but it is a good idea to import the image into Photoshop and compare it with the original (this presumes that your computer system is correctly calibrated as discussed on page 48). If the original is a print or piece of flat artwork, view it in neutral light, such as that coming from a color-corrected lighting system or (the most practical option) daylight. Slides should be compared by illuminating them on a lightbox (Remember to use the appropriate light source for illlumination).

Check the Histogram (select *Image* > **Histogram**) and assess the distribution of levels within the image. A well exposed "normal" image will comprise a bell-curved shaped Gaussian distribution. In practice, the predominance of tones from, say, the sky, will affect the distribution.

❶ The *Histogram* feature is an excellent way to quickly check the tonal range of an image.

❷❸ When images are scanned the results are often lacking in contrast. By using Photoshop's *Levels* command (*Adjust* > **Levels**) we can see that the tones are not equally distributed throughout the image.

❹❺ The corrected image has a full range of tones and exhibits much better contrast. We could use Photoshop's automatic controls to achieve this (using the *Auto Levels* or *Auto Contrast* commands) or adjust the levels themselves

❻❼ Using software such as the ICE[3] suite during a scan is an excellent and expedient way of getting a "clean" scan as these "with" and "without" illustrations show.

❶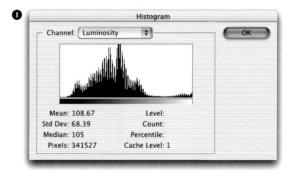

❷

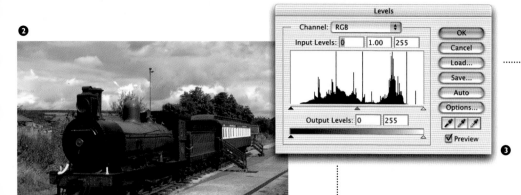

❸

❹

❺

Look out particularly for an absence of levels at the top and bottom of the distribution. This would show there to be no real blacks (if the gap is to the left) or whites (to the right). We can correct this by using the *Levels* command. Open the *Levels* dialog box (*Image > Adjust > **Levels***) and move the sliders below the histogram to the end of the tonal distributions at the black and white ends respectively.

Finally examine the image for sharpness. If the image is not critically sharp, use the *Unsharp Mask* filter (page 86) to make corrections.

Using a Slide Scanner

Slide scanners—and their respective software—are used in much the same manner as a flatbed. The smaller size of transparencies or negatives makes cleanliness more important, but most slide scanners feature dust- and scratch-removal software. If you have a number of slides to scan, some models feature automatic batch processing that can speed up (and automate) the process.

Newton's rings

Should your original be a glossy print photograph then there's a chance of thin film interference when you place it on the scanner's glass plate. Better known as Newton's Rings, it is worth attending to this at the scanning stage. Ensuring that there is no moisture on either the print or plate can sometimes remedy the condition, otherwise a card mount under the print can keep the surfaces apart.

❻

❼

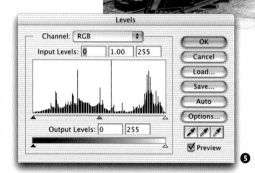

44

PHOTOSHOP'S COMPUTER REQUIREMENTS

Any time devoted to setting up and optimizing your computer and its peripherals will be time well spent. Even if your system has been performing to your complete satisfaction there are a few tricks and fixes that could really make it fly.

The computer and computing platforms

Like all digital manipulation and graphics applications, Photoshop makes extreme demands on your computer system. This is due to the fundamental process of image editing. Any image file stored as a bitmap will already be large as file sizes go. When you then apply a manipulation, transformation, or other effects to that image the processes, which involve applying mathematical calculations to each and every pixel, demand considerable computing power.

It is often said that for digital imaging you need the most powerful computer you can afford. While in the broadest sense this is true, such a generalization overlooks two important factors.

First, many of you reading this book will already have a computer and second, power and performance don't necessarily equate.

Apple Macintosh OS X operating system

Processor speed is often quoted as being the premier indicator of performance and, as a guideline, it is a useful parameter. But ultimate performance will be influenced by the speed of the computer's infrastructure, which enables data and commands to be passed between devices and the RAM (Random Access Memory) provided. Remember that MHz—and increasingly GHz—clock speeds do not equate across all platforms. For example, Macintosh computers of a given clock speed, due to their different architecture, will offer performance equivalent to a Windows PC with nearly twice the clock speed.

For Photoshop performance the amount of RAM is probably the most significant factor. Its developer, Adobe, suggests comparatively modest amounts of RAM for running Photoshop, but its users suggest far greater amounts. Realistically you'd be wise to consider an amount of RAM equivalent to around four times the size of the typical images you are working on. And this should be in addition to the requirements of the operating system. It's a case of more is better. With this amount of RAM your computer will be able to retain the image in memory even as you add layers, channels, and maintain multiple undos.

But what about Virtual Memory? Virtual Memory, for those who have not encountered this "dodge" before, is an area of hard disk that is used as if it were additional RAM. Therefore for a computer with 256MB of RAM, an equivalent amount of Virtual Memory will give the computer an apparent

---

T I P

Video cards

The computer's video card is an often neglected part of the performance chain. Responsible for drawing and refreshing the screen it needs to support your monitor's resolution, scan rate, and color bit-depth. In many computers these are fixed but where you have the option of upgrading the card you may find this is an economical way of boosting the performance of the computer.

Windows XP operating system

allocation of 512MB. This is a good way of expanding memory, but it does come at a price. Data stored in Virtual Memory needs to be written to and read from the hard disk as and when needed. Although this is a fast process, it is a little slower than using "real" RAM.

Platform wars

So which is best, Mac or PC? That's a perennial question with no clear answer. And for most of us the outcome will be determined by which computer we already own and are familiar with. With regard to Photoshop your general preference is still likely to hold sway. Only if you are being pedantic will you find hard and fast distinctions.

The Windows user will point to the wide use of Windows-based PCs. There is also a far greater range of software available and often both hardware and software are less expensive than Mac alternatives. However, Mac users will bring up the graphics professionals' preference for the Mac platform. They will also tell you how the setting up of peripherals and calibration of monitors is both simpler and more accurate. And, perhaps controversially, they'll tell you how much easier to use and how robust the Mac Operating System is. Some prejudice against Windows dates from when a number of software packages were originally designed for the Mac, and the first Windows versions were buggy and unreliable. For the purposes of this book, either platform will do.

Memory manipulations – Macintosh

The Mac operating system's (OS 9 and earlier) *Get Info* panel lets you set enhanced memory levels for the application. Select the Photoshop application icon and then *File > Get Info > Memory* and type in a new amount. You can increase the amount of virtual memory using the *Memory Control Panel*. If you use OS X, then virtual memory is actively managed by it and should not be adjusted.

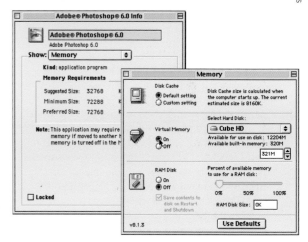

Memory manipulations – Windows

You can use the *System Properties > Performance* control panel in Windows to alter the amount of memory made available to Photoshop (or any other application). When you select "Let me specify my own memory" settings you can increase the amount allocated to it. Note that this will be Virtual Memory.

46 Monitor performance

The standard monitors supplied with many computers are quite adequate but, designed as they are for those who will mainly be using them for word processing and games, absolute color fidelity is rarely considered important. However, for the photographer and graphics professional that fidelity must be a prerequisite. You need to have the confidence that whatever you create on screen will, when posted to the Web or printed, look pretty much the same. And, as with so many things in life, when it comes to monitors bigger is better.

It is worth taking a moment to discuss monitor safety. The human eye was not designed for many of the uses to which we put it today; staring at a computer monitor is an obvious example. While any extended use of a monitor could contribute to problems, the use of image editing software is likely to put a significant strain on our eyes. The best advice—which is not always easily heeded—is to avoid prolonged periods at the screen. Take short breaks, and if headaches become regular, check that you are sitting at least arms length from the screen and have your eyesight checked out by an appropriate optician.

There is good reason not to use old monitors. First, all monitors' color performance changes with age—often imperceptibly—but enough to make accurate calibration impossible. Second, and more important on health grounds, some older monitors have poor screen refresh rates. In simple terms, the screen flicker gets worse. You may not notice the flicker, but your brain will! Later models have high refresh rates that reduce flicker to an imperceptible

amount. Here's a tip to see if your screen is suffering from flicker. Open a word processing application (so the computer monitor screen is mostly white) and hold a sheet of white paper with a black cross in the center over the screen. Move the paper to one side and keep your eye on the cross. When the monitor is at the edge of your vision you will see it pulse visibly if it has a low refresh rate.

When looking for a new monitor (or assessing the performance of your existing model) the points to look most closely at are:

Size

Many people use 14-inch monitors successfully but a 17-inch model gives you substantially more workspace, and these days such monitors are also very competetively priced.

Resolution

The bonus in having a larger monitor is that it can display a larger workspace; in other words, it offers increased resolution. While a 14-inch monitor may comfortably display a screen resolution of 640 x 480 pixels, a 17-inch monitor (or a 15-inch LCD model) may offer resolutions as high as 1,024 x 768 pixels.

Color Depth

Images, even if ultimately destined for the confines of the Web, need as many colors as possible to be displayed accurately and to avoid dithering artifacts. True Color (24 bit, 16.7 million colors) is essential. This is called Millions of Colors on Macintosh computers.

1

Windows Description	Macintosh Description	Number of colors displayed	Overall Bit-depth
Bitmap	-	2	1
Grayscale	256 Grays	256	8
Indexed color (256 Colors)	256 Colors	256	8
High Color	Thousands of Colors	65,000	16
True Color	Millions of Colors	16.7 million	24

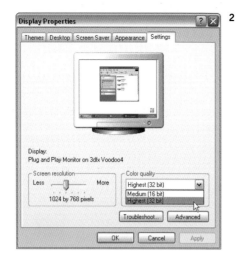

1 *Monitor colors compared.*

2 *You can alter the bit-depth of your computer very simply. On Windows computers use the Display Control Panel (you can also change the screen resolution here).*

3|4 *On Macintosh computers (OS 9 and earlier) use the equivalent Monitors Control Panel (or the pop up on the Power Bar). OS X users need to select System Preferences from the Dock and then Displays (or use the more limited option on the Dock itself).*

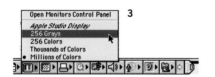

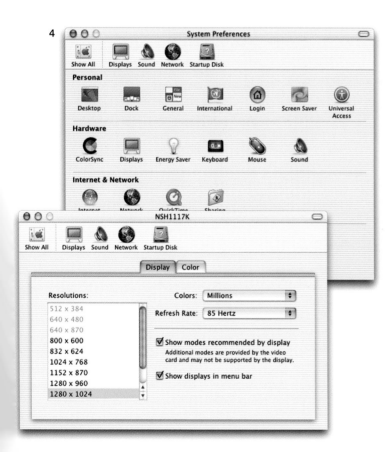

Most of us will have heard of other health risks associated with monitor use, in particular low-frequency radiation. Claim and counterclaim have been made and it is probably wise to assume that there is some substance in people's concern. But as always, good sense should come to the fore. If you keep at a good distance from your screen and take breaks, you are lessening any risk. Specialized screens that claim to offer protection may help, but many tests have only revealed that emissions from the screen itself are less than those from the back and sides of the monitor. However, many such screens are effective at improving screen contrast and reducing reflection. But if you have invested in an LCD screen, then there is virtually no risk. LCD monitors are powered by fluorescent sources similar to those used in lightbulbs.

Conventional versus flat displays

The fact that traditional cathode ray tube monitors are, by nature, particularly bulky has been one of the drivers behind the creation of flat panel displays. These newcomers may offer compactness (and succeed in returning your desktop to you) but is their quality good enough for image manipulation? The answer has to be a conditional yes, and as the technology improves we're likely to see more and more LCD displays rivaling the top-quality traditional models made by Apple, Silicon Graphics, and others.

Does quality matter?

But do you need truly accurate color displays if your computer is mainly destined for Web work, especially as your results will only be as good as the monitors on which other people see your pictures? Arguably not, but that's no reason to compromise. You need to ensure that anything you output is of the highest quality. And if you've purchased Photoshop, it is unlikely that your computer will be used solely for Web creations.

48 Monitor calibrations

All monitors—certainly all those of the same model from a particular manufacturer—are created equal. That would suggest that each should perform in exactly the same way and deliver identical results. However, if you view two monitors, identical in all respects and set up in exactly the same way, you'll probably notice distinct differences in the way identical images are represented on screen. Which of them is correct? Probably neither!

To ensure that an image on your monitor is displayed correctly (as close as possible to the original color, contrast, and brightness), you need to calibrate the monitor. As part of this process you need to ensure the linearity is correct—that the image is the correct shape with squares displayed as squares and circles neither elliptical or egg-shaped.

Fortunately, because you'll be working in a closed system (one in which you have complete control over the image acquisition, manipulation and output), you can take a few shortcuts and still achieve very acceptable results. You can use the calibration software provided with your computer's operating system and that found within Photoshop.

Gamma, gamut, and color space explained

The range of colors that can reproduce color on a monitor is known as the color space and varies, due to the manufacturing process, from monitor to monitor. The extent of this color space is called the Gamut. Calibration (see page 48) is used to try and limit the differences between devices (which include printers where appropriate). The term Gamma describes the extent of the contrast in the midtones (or, more specifically, the midtone grays) in an image. The Gamma setting determines the lightness or darkness of these midtones. The default gamma setting for a Macintosh is 1.8 while for a Windows PC it is 2.2. The net result is that an image displayed on a Windows PC will look darker than on a Mac. We will see later how to preview the differences between monitors so you can decide if it's worthwhile compensating now for the Gamma of monitors on which your work will be seen later.

Calibrating your monitor

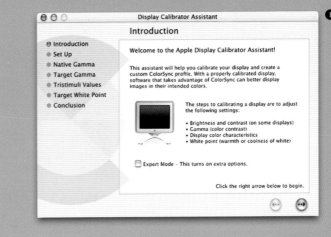

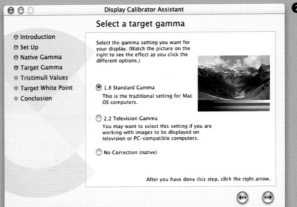

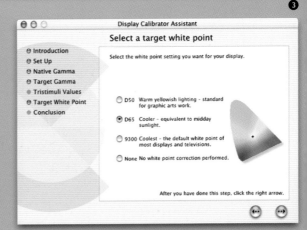

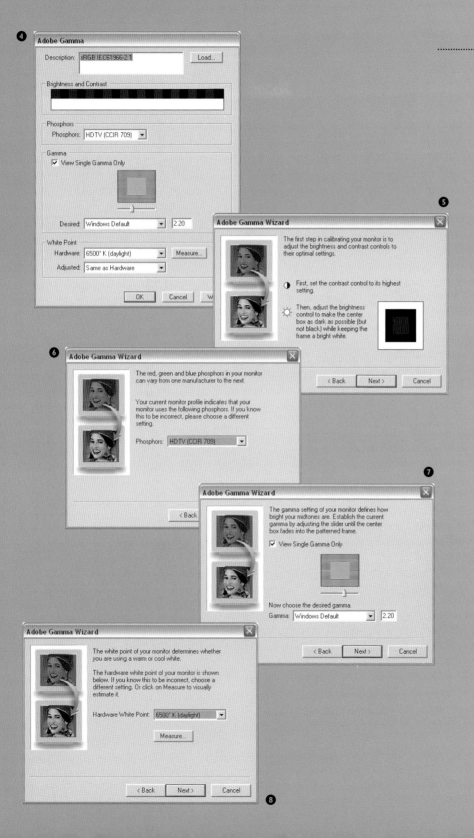

1 Mac users can use the *Monitor Calibration Assistant* to work through screen calibration stages. Select the *Monitors* control panel (or *Displays* in OS X) then press the *Color* button and select *Calibrate*.

2 First, you'll be asked to set the Gamma. Unless you have any reason to change it, it is best to leave this on its default setting (Standard).

3 Next set the white point. The default D65 (sometimes shown as 6,500K) is a good compromise.

Finally, if you have made any changes, you'll be asked to name your specific calibration and then save it.

The Adobe *Gamma Control Panel* (on both Windows and Mac) offers another easy calibration regime and is put in place during the Photoshop installation.

4 Open the Adobe Gamma and you have the choice of an *Assistant*, which will take you through each stage, or a single control panel in which you can set the same values.

5 Using the *Assistant*, make adjustments to the brightness and contrast.

6 Next, select a set of screen phosphors that are the closest match to those of your monitor. (If you are unsure then it's best to use the default values.)

7 Set the Gamma by altering the sliders under each of the color panes until the center and frame appear equally bright.

8 Finally set the white point. As before, 6,500K is a good value. Finally, Save.

50 INSTALLING AND OPTIMIZING PHOTOSHOP FOR THE WEB

There is nothing particularly onerous about installing Photoshop. The process will ask for your product serial number and request an installation type: Compact, Custom, or Typical. It's best—unless you have any pressing need to do otherwise—to select Typical.

Setting preferences

Once installation is complete it makes good sense, as well as good working practice, to set identical preferences for both Photoshop and ImageReady. (This will ensure a good workflow and prevent errors due to assumptions about individual settings in each.) Preferences are settings that are applied to the application (rather than to individual files). You can open the *Preferences* dialog by selecting *Edit* > *Preferences* > **General**, which gives you the general preferences, and use the dropdown menu to select different panes.

3

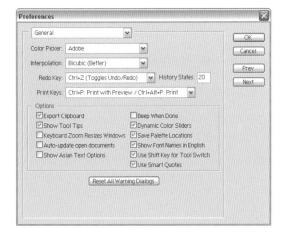

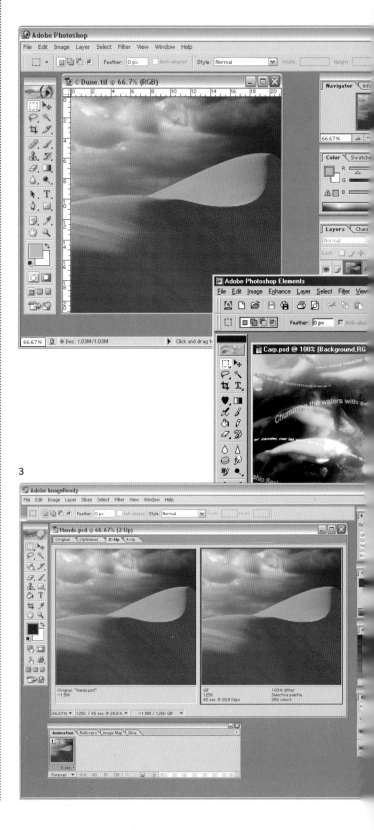

1

The Photoshop interface is almost infinitely customizable so the views shown here reflect the default setting, as it would appear before any changes have been made.

1 *Photoshop 7*

2 *Photoshop Elements*

3 *Adobe ImageReady*

4 *Photoshop 6 (Macintosh Version)*

2

Rectangular Marquee

Selects a rectangular area of an image. The selected area can then

4

Geometries

MP2 optimized geometry

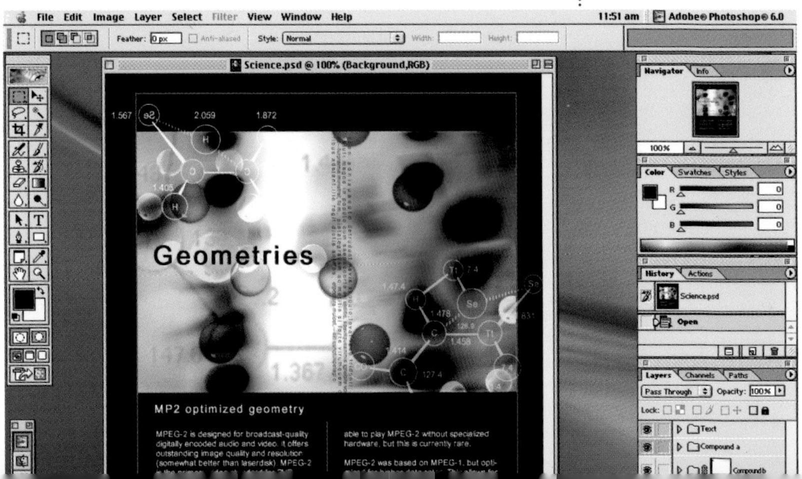

Here are some suggestions for useful Preference settings (note that many of these are defaults).

General preferences
- *Color Picker*: Adobe. It is as good as any, and is the one used in this book.
- *Interpolation*: Bicubic. The better of the methods, if not the fastest.
- *History States*: At least 20. More is preferable, but it consumes more memory.

Preferences for saving files
- *Image Previews*: Always Save. Note, however, that this can add as much as 25 percent to a file size, but that saving previews does make the task of finding images easier.
- *Select Icon*: Windows Thumbnail, Macintosh Thumbnail.
- *Append File Extension*: Always. Although not strictly necessary for Macintosh users, it is helpful in Web work to be able to see the extension that identifies the file type.
- *Recent File List*: Depends on how many files you typically work with. If you intend to create GIF Animations you may need higher numbers for convenience. A figure between four and ten is probably ideal.

Preferences for display and cursors
- Select *Brush Size* for painting cursors and *Precise* for others. These settings let you see the extent of a paint tool and allow precision when making object selections. The alternative tool-shaped cursors are almost without exception unsatisfactory.
  - Use *Pixel Doubling*: (Photoshop only) Turn this on only if speed is a problem; it lets Photoshop create lower-resolution previews (though any effect applied is at full resolution).

Preference for units and rulers
- Pixels are the ideal measurement unit in which to work.

52 Photoshop palettes

Photoshop features a range of floating palettes that can be placed anywhere on screen or dropped into the *Palette Well* to preserve workspace.

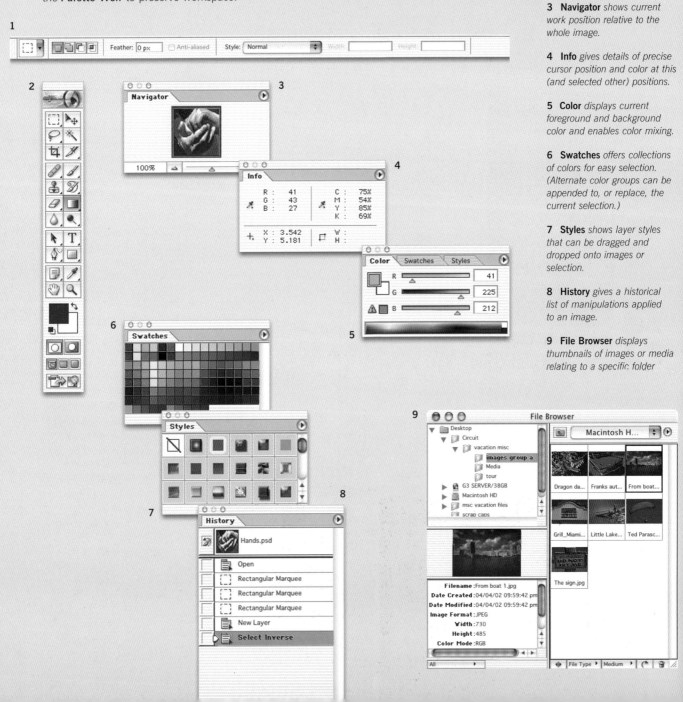

1 **Tool Options** *are shown in the context-sensitive* Tool Options *bar (here showing the options for the* Rectangular Marquee*).*

2 **The Toolbox** *is home to the Photoshop Tools.*

3 **Navigator** *shows current work position relative to the whole image.*

4 **Info** *gives details of precise cursor position and color at this (and selected other) positions.*

5 **Color** *displays current foreground and background color and enables color mixing.*

6 **Swatches** *offers collections of colors for easy selection. (Alternate color groups can be appended to, or replace, the current selection.)*

7 **Styles** *shows layer styles that can be dragged and dropped onto images or selection.*

8 **History** *gives a historical list of manipulations applied to an image.*

9 **File Browser** *displays thumbnails of images or media relating to a specific folder*

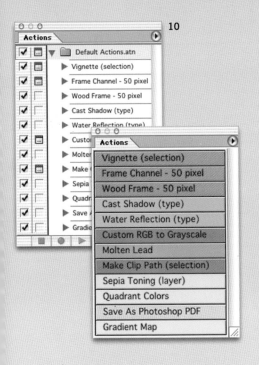

10 Actions *(can be displayed as listing or buttons). A list of Actions (macros) can be used to automate edits.*

11 Layers *displays details of the layers in an image.*

12 Channels *displays image channels.*

13 Paths *Shows paths connected with the selected image (if any).*

14 Character, Paragraph *Gives information on text and layout.*

15 *The* Palette Well

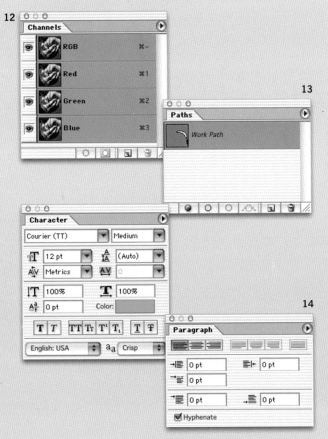

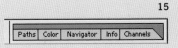

Using The Palette Well

From Photoshop version 6 (and including Photoshop Elements) onward, the floating palettes can be "docked" in a *Palette Well* that can be found to the right of the *Tool Options* bar. Palette tabs are dragged to the *Palette Well* to place them in the well. Clicking on the appropriate palette name in the well will temporarily open the palette (for example to select a color from the *Swatches* palette or a style from the *Styles* palette). To open a palette and to make it available again as a floating palette click first on the name of the palette then drag it away from the well.

Remeber that if you use Photoshop in Windows or Macintosh OS at a screen resolution of 800 x 600 pixels the *Palette Well* will not be visible. However, you can (at any screen resolution) hide and show palettes using the *Window* menu.

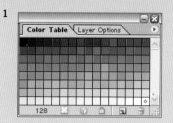

54 ImageReady palettes

ImageReady shares many palettes with Photoshop.
Listed here are the features unique to ImageReady:

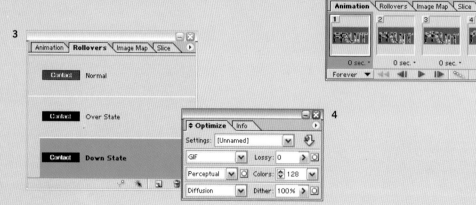

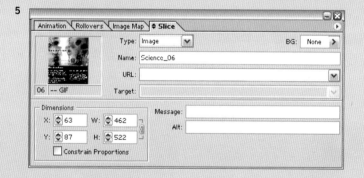

1 Color *Table shows colors used in the selected image.*

2 Animation *displays GIF Animations.*

3 Rollover *shows rollover components.*

4 Optimize *displays optimization data.*

5 Slices *Displays data relating to image slices.*

6 Image Map *displays data relating to image map constructs.*

7 Toolbox *The ImageReady toolbox features a similar layout to that of Photoshop, with just a few changes. Most notable is the* View in Browser *button, which is discussed later.*

Photoshop Elements palettes

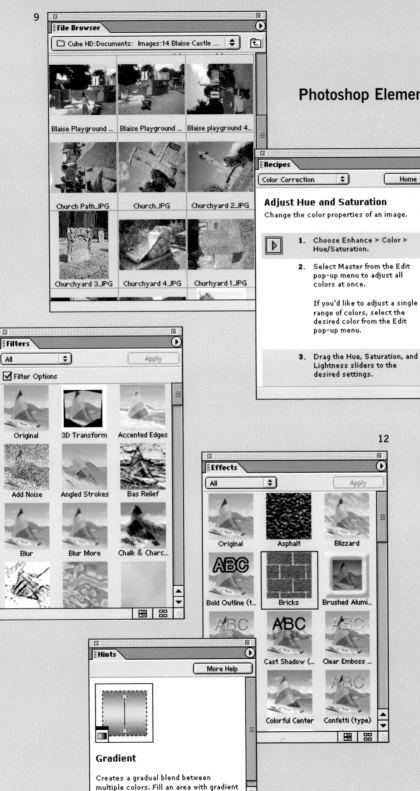

8 Toolbox *The Photoshop Elements is similar to that of Photoshop.*

9 File Browser *displays thumbnails of images or media for a selected folder.*

Here are the features unique to Photoshop Elements:

10 Recipes *gives step-by-step instructions for common image manipulations.*

11 Filters Browser *displays filter effects as applied to a thumbnail image.*

12 Effects Browser *displays image effects as applied to a thumbnail.*

13 Hints *gives context-sensitive assistance relating to the currently selected tool or feature.*

SPEAKING THE WEB LANGUAGE

Before you get down to creating your winning Web graphics, take a little time to review some of the terms that are used extensively over the next few chapters.

Webpage

Rarely a single image or graphic, a webpage is typically composed of multiple elements that are arranged and positioned by the HTML code that describes the page. There are no absolute dimensions to a webpage. It could, in theory, be any size. In practice you need to be mindful of those who will visit the site, and create a page that can easily fit on their screens, preferably with no scrolling (unless you're designing a major news site). Size is not necessarily a limitation—it is often more effective to present information or images in compact chunks.

URL

A URL, or Uniform Resource Locator, is the unique address of a website or webpage. The URL of the current webpage displayed by the browser will be displayed in the window across the top. Most URLs are preceded by http://.

2

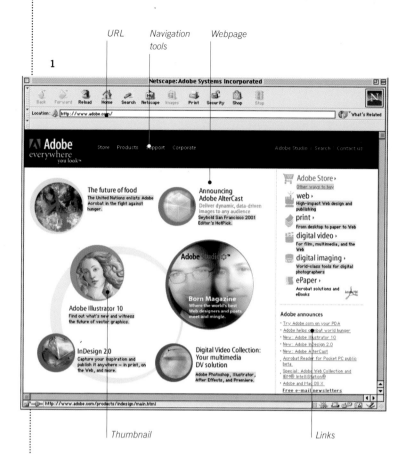

1

URL   Navigation tools   Webpage

Thumbnail   Links

Links

Often indicated in blue or red (through convention rather than rule) and underlined or contained within buttons, links take the website visitor off to an associated location. For example, by pressing the Home button on a website you will be taken to the homepage. When you select any link the appropriate file or URL is downloaded to your browser. That URL might be part of the currently viewed website, or of any other.

Navigation tools

Navigation tools—which may be buttons, conventional links, or a toolbox—are essential to make your visitors comfortable within your website. They enable easy negotiation of the site, including fast access to principal areas and the homepage. It's a good idea to feature some navigational aid on every page. Don't rely on the browser's back button to take the lost homeward!

TIP

Remember to use text too!

It seems ironic to mention text in a book devoted to Web graphics, but an image map should always be accompanied by the same options in plain text because visitors may have set their browser not to display graphics. In this setting they would not be able to proceed past the current page.

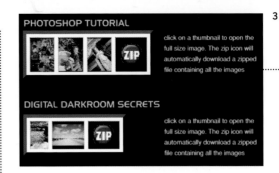

Thumbnail

Thumbnails are small, low-resolution images used as previews on a website. Often these comprise links to another part of the site where a higher resolution or larger version of the image can be viewed or downloaded. Thumbnails are very useful because of their compact size, which makes them easy to download.

Image maps

An image map is a single image that contains multiple links to other webpages in the current site, or to independent URLs. Image maps are often used within the homepage as a "launch pad" to separate areas of the website. Such a map is a neat way of combining several links into a compact space. Because they are single large graphics, rollovers (see below) don't work with image maps.

Rollovers

The term rollover can describe any button, icon, graphic, or image that changes when the mouse pointer moves over it. A rollover works by having two identically sized images. One is the normal "Off" image. This is what you would see when the page first opens. The second "On" image appears when the mouse rolls over or onto it. Rollovers can be both effective and practically useful where, for instance, further information is displayed when a thumbnail is rolled over.

4 Rollovers are a simple way of creating an interactive experience for your visitors.

5 A single image can be sliced into sections (invisibly), and have links attached to each.

6 ImageReady allows you to prepare simple animations using a succession of images.

Image slices

Use image slices (or, more simply, slices) to divide an image or document into smaller selections that can be treated as separate elements and optimized individually. Different optimization settings can be used, if necessary, for each slice. When an image is sliced, each slice—a rectangular pane of the image —can automatically generate a corresponding HTML file using ImageReady.

Animation

We've already mentioned animations briefly with respect to the GIF file type. Using ImageReady you can create and edit animations from a set of source images. Animations are an excellent way of adding a dynamic element to your website without adding significantly to the file download.

1 The basic elements of any webpage: the URL, a navigation menu, links and thumbnails.

2 A set of links at the foot of a webpage can take visitors directly to related information.

3 Links can be made more attractive by putting them in thumbnail images.

5

6

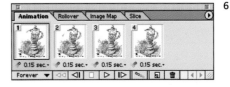

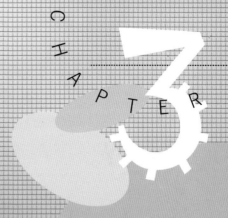

Basic Image Manipulations

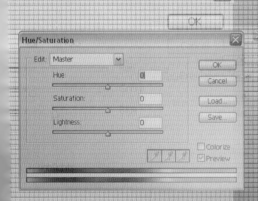

In this section we will explore the features and techniques needed to make basic image corrections and manipulations. There is an enormous range of tools and commands in Photoshop, which can sometimes be intimidating. We'll tackle some of the more important ones here.

It would be a good idea to work with your own images alongside the examples provided in this chapter. Although you will rarely do anything that might have a catastrophic or irreversible impact on the image, it is always good practice to work on a copy of an image rather than the image itself!

60 CROPPING AND RESIZING

Taking cues from the traditional darkroom, Photoshop gives you various methods of cropping and resizing your images. You can even alter the perspective of your image during the crop, to correct errors or lens distortions that might have been introduced when you took the photographs. You will have little of the hard grind of a real-world darkroom, but results that are just as professional.

Cropping

Cropping involves trimming the physical dimensions of the original image to remove unwanted elements or alter the composition of the image.

Begin by opening your image. Select *File > Open* and then select the image from the appropriate directory and menu. If the image you select is smaller or larger than the space on the desktop, use the *Zoom* tool (the magnifying glass on the toolbox) to enlarge or reduce the size. Alternatively, select *View > Fit to Window* for the optimum size.

❶ Select the *Crop* tool and drag from the top left of your intended selection to the bottom right. Note that, when you release the mouse button, the area outside the cropped area darkens. This darkening can be altered in color and opacity or removed altogether using the controls on the *Tool Option* bar.

❷ Where it is important that a crop is of a precise size (for example if you intend it to fill a predetermined space on a webpage) the required dimensions can be entered on the *Tool Options* bar, along with your required resolution.

❸ To match the dimensions and resolution of an existing image select that image and click the *Front Image* button. Now when the *Crop* tool is applied to the new image it will conform to the format of the existing image.

❹❺❻ Less precise crop adjustments can be achieved by dragging the handles (the small squares at the corners or the mid-points of the sides). The cropped area can now also be rotated (by fine or coarse amounts) by moving the cursor to the cropped area.

The crop selection can be rotated prior to application of the crop. Alignment is made considerably easier this way.

TIP

Rectangular Marquee

The *Rectangular Marquee* can also be used as a crop tool, although it is nominally used to select areas so there's no border shading.

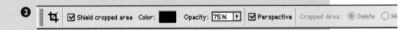

Perspective cropping

❶ You can crop your image to take account of (and correct) perspective effects in an image. Where an image features distortion, as it does here, (normally because the camera has been tilted) the resulting converging verticals or horizontals can be corrected.

❷ Before applying your crop click the *Perspective* box on the *Tool Options* bar.

❸ Move the corner handles to compensate for the problem. The image itself will not be corrected as you do this, so it is a good idea to align the crop edges with verticals or horizontals in the image.

❹ Apply the crop. Note that correcting converging verticals can sometimes produce an image that appears stretched vertically. To maintain the image's proportions you may need to flatten it slightly, by pulling the top handle downward prior to cropping.

Precise cursors

The default installation of Photoshop results in tool cursors being represented by small, representative icons. If you need more precision, select *Edit > Preferences > **Display and Cursors*** and choose the *Precise Cursor* options. The cursors then become more precise, which enables accurate positioning.

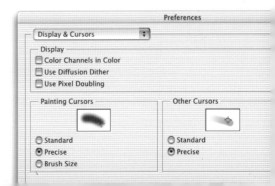

62   Resizing

Given the apparently limitless sources of images it is very unlikely that any image will be the correct size for your application when you first acquire it. In most cases, therefore, you will need to resize the image.

In Photoshop the *Image Size* (*Image* > *Image Size*) command gives you the opportunity to specify a new size by giving new pixel dimensions (or physical dimensions) and altering the resolution. For Web purposes you can ignore the physical dimension settings and set the resolution to 72dpi.

Although resizing is not a difficult process, Adobe has thoughtfully provided an 'assistant' (called a *Wizard*) that can help you achieve the resizing.

Using the *Wizard* creates a copy of the original image; the original is preserved at its original size and resolution. But when using the menu command *Image Size*, no copy is made.

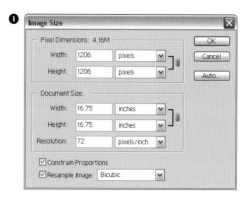

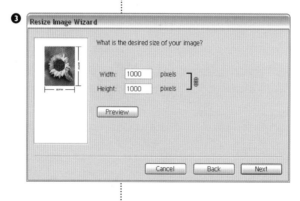

❶ The resize box allows you to change the resolution and absolute dimension. Note the original and new file sizes, which are indicated at the top of the box.

❷ You'll find the resize assistant by selecting *Help* > *Resize Image*.

Select *Online* as the intended application.

❸ Enter the new pixel dimensions. Note that you need only enter either the horizontal or vertical resolution. The other resolution will be adjusted automatically for you.

❹ That's it. The final screen provides useful advice about sharpening the image (since resizing can sometimes compromise image sharpness).

① Select the *Canvas Size* command.

② To expand to the right, click on the left center box and add the new pixel width in the box. (You could also enlarge the area above and below the current space by typing in a new height for the canvas.)

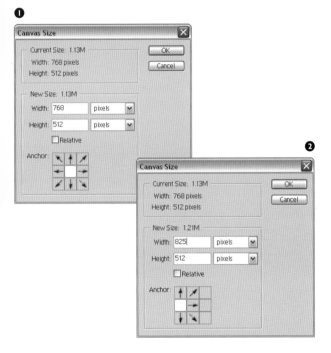

Changing aspect ratios

By default, changes to the image size are proportional: the original aspect ratio (the ratio of height to width) is preserved. To change the aspect ratio (for example, to flatten or narrow an image slightly to fill an existing space), click on the *Constrain Proportions* box to remove the tick you will find in the box there. You'll then need to provide both a new width and a new height.

Canvas size

The *Canvas Size* command (*Image* > **Canvas Size**) is useful if you need to expand the image space without altering the size of the image itself. This could, for example, be the case if you have an existing image (perhaps the principal graphic for your webpage), but need to add space to the right to put some navigation buttons in place. You can use the *Canvas Size* command to expand the canvas to the right.

Some new best friends

When you've completed the exercises later in this section and are preparing your work for the Web, there are two features that you are not likely to have come across before. Indicated by an innocuous box at the base of the Photoshop toolbox, *Jump To* lets you transfer your current work directly between Photoshop and ImageReady. Similarly, from ImageReady you can jump to Photoshop. You can also automatically update files or documents when jumping between Photoshop and ImageReady. In Photoshop choose *Edit* > *Preferences* > **General**, then select **Auto-update Open Documents**. In ImageReady choose *Edit* > *Preferences* > **General**, then select the **Auto-Update Files** option.

The second feature is *Preview in Default Browser*. This enables you to quickly view your work as it is being interpreted by any Web browser that may be installed on your computer. In Photoshop select *File* > **Save for Web**, then choose a browser from the *Preview In* button at the bottom right area of the *Save for Web* window.

64 MAKING COLOR AND TONAL ADJUSTMENTS

After cropping your "raw" image to the proportions you require, the next fixes are likely to involve ensuring that the color, brightness, and contrast of your images are correctly set.

A good analogy would be to compare these adjustments with their direct equivalents on a television. To get an ideal picture often involves not only setting all three controls, but also readjusting them until your ideal is realized. Like many aspects of Photoshop there are both simple (crude) and more thorough ways of achieving these corrections.

1 *Color controls (known as* Saturation *in Photoshop) adjust the color saturation from being completely unsaturated (that is, a black and white image) through to full saturation (when colors take on a garish glow).*

2 *When adjusting contrast you've the option of altering the contrast from low (when there will be little distinction between light and dark parts of the image) to high. At this latter setting there are few intermediate tones, since most of the image is represented in black and white.*

3 *The more obvious* Brightness *is self-explanatory. Play around with it until you are happy with the results.*

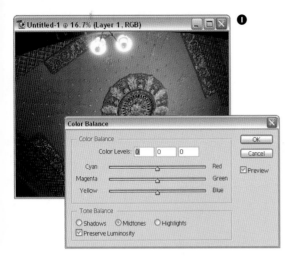

Color adjustments

Many circumstances contribute to an image having colors that are not authentic, leading to the color balance looking unnatural in some way. If the image was originally shot using a conventional camera, daylight balance film might have been used to shoot indoors. If a digital camera was used its white balance may have been set to that of an alternative lighting source to ambient. In either case you can make corrections easily using the *Color Balance* control. This control, comprising three sliders, lets you reduce (or increase) the amount of each individual color. It shifts the balance between the chosen color and its compliment: red and cyan, magenta and green or blue and yellow.

In Photoshop Elements there is a fast fix for color balance: *Color Cast* (*Enhance* > *Color* > **Color Cast**). This works by asking you to identify a neutral element in the scene and automatically adjusts the color balance to neutralize any casts. It is particularly effective in most —but not all—cases of color casting.

❶ Open your image and select the *Color Balance* command (*Image* > *Adjust* > **Color Balance**).

To correct an image (such as this, which has an amber, tungsten lighting cast concealing the aqua-colored ceiling), you need to reduce the cyan and yellow components of the image and, to a lesser degree, the magenta.

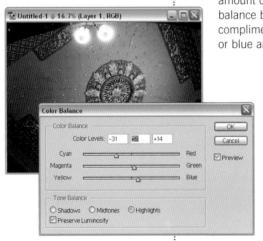

❷ Use the sliders to make these corrections, monitoring the effect on the image.

❸ You now need to assess the image. Making corrections is easier if there are some areas of neutral tone in the image. Take note of any areas you know to be gray, white, or black. Do they exhibit a color bias? If so, make corrections to neutralize them (for example, by reducing the magenta to remove a pink cast).

❹ When you are happy with the results click *OK* to apply the effect to the image.

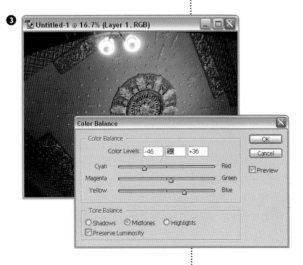

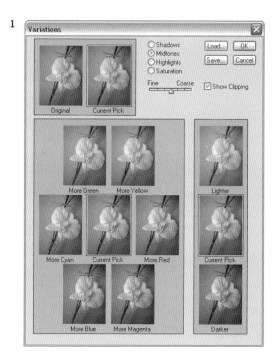

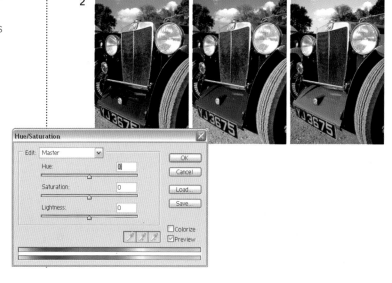

1 Variations *creates thumbnails of color balance contrast, and saturation alternatives to your original*

2 *The* Hue, Saturation *and* Brightness *sliders enable you to make instant adustments, with a preview option*

66 Variations

The Variations feature is a useful way of assessing and correcting not only color balance but contrast and saturation too. The *Variations* command (*Image > Adjust > Variation* in Photoshop and *Enhance > Variations* in Photoshop Elements) presents your current image as a thumbnail surrounded by alternatives with different color balances, contrasts and saturations. It is comparatively easy to correct your image by clicking on whichever thumbnail offers the best characteristics.

Hue and Saturation

The *Hue/Saturation* command (*Image > Adjust > Hue Saturation*) lets you alter the hues in your image, as well as their saturation, by means of intuitive slider controls.

Altering the *Hue* slider changes all the hues in your image according to a spectral sequence based on a 360-degree spectrum. Here our original image has been adjusted by moving the slider by a 120-degree increment. In most cases, you would only use this control when changing the hue setting of part of an image, for example when altering the blue of a sky from cyan to true blue.

The *Saturation* command, by comparison, merely alters the color saturation. The *Lightness* control (which has the same function as the lightness slider in the *Brightness/Contrast* dialog box) can be used to lighten or darken the image after making changes to the hue and saturation if required.

❶

❷

Toned images

The Colorize box in the Hue/Saturation dialog box provides a useful means of producing toned images. Such images can be used effectively as Web graphics or, by fading them with the Lightness control, as backgrounds.

❻

❸

❶❷ Click the *Colorize* box. If the image turns a salmon-pink color, don't worry: this is normal.

❸❹ Move the *Hue* slider to alter the hue. Traditional sepia and selenium tones are possible, along with a range of more "dayglo" intermediates.

❺❻ Alter the saturation for a more subtle effect and, if required, increase the brightness to create a background image.

❹

❺

68 Exploring the Levels palette

The *Levels* command displays the histogram of the
active image in the *Levels* dialog box. This maps
the pixels in an image to one of 255 color-intensity
levels. It is a good indication of whether an image
has enough details in each of the highlights (to the
right of the graph), shadows (to the left) and midtones (central portion) to enable effective corrections
to be made without making the image look messy.

Sliders on the *Levels* palette let you alter the white,
black, and midpoints to achieve a better distribution
of levels throughout the image.

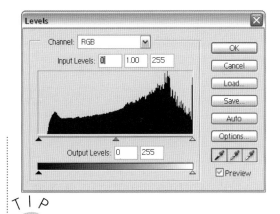

T I P

Automatic corrections

Photoshop offers three shortcuts for image fixing:
Auto Levels, Auto Contrast and *Auto Color*. Auto
Levels moves the Levels sliders automatically to set
highlight and shadow locations, defining the lightest
and darkest pixels in the image as white and black
respectively. Intermediate pixels are distributed
proportionately. This is ideal for images that can
be described as "normal", i.e. featuring an average
distribution of pixel values. It can also be effective
for removing color casts. However, when a specific
color cast is intended or the distribution of pixels
is not average, the more precise *Levels* command
should be used instead. Similarly, *Auto Contrast*
makes corrections based on average contrast
values. These may or may not correspond to those
of the image. For a quick fix it is often worth using
these commands. But if the results are not as
expected, or they fail to improve the image, use
the conventional fixes.

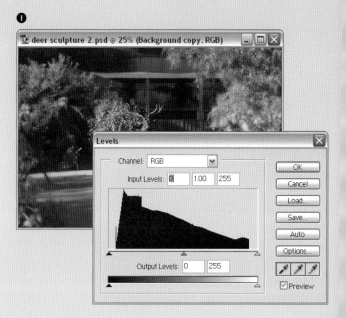

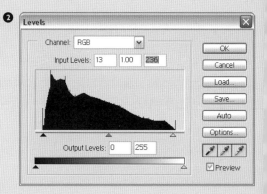

69

Exploring the Levels palette

❸

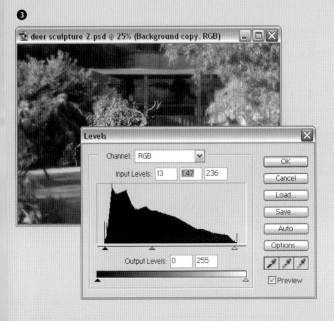

❹

❶ Begin by opening your image and the *Levels* dialog (*Image > Adjust > **Levels*** in Photoshop Enhance, or *Brightness/Contrast > **Levels*** in Photoshop Elements).

This image is missing some tones at the white end and has a slightly compressed contrast range.

❷ Move the outermost sliders to the start and end of the levels on the histogram. If there are any extreme levels (i.e. not part of the curve) these can usually be ignored.

❸ Move the central (mid-tones) slider so that it bisects the area under the curve. (This is a rule of thumb; you may need to adjust the position either side of this slightly to get the best midtone response.)

❹ Here's our image with its levels corrected.

Using the lower *Output* Levels sliders, drawing each toward the center slightly can reduce the contrast in an image.

70 THE SELECTION TOOLS

The *Selection* tools are a group of tools found on the toolbar, which are designed to enable the selections of parts of an image based on different criteria. When one of these tools is used, the selected parts of the image become "active". You can then apply manipulations and effects to your selection, or copy the selected area (for use as a component in a montage, for example).

The *Marquee* is the basic selection tool. It is a shape-based tool that makes selections based on either rectangular or elliptical forms. Additional options are provided to enable a single vertical column or horizontal row of pixels to be selected.

The *Lasso* enables the selection of irregular shapes using a freehand tool to enclose a selection. The *Magnetic* variant automatically follows the perimeter of an object, while the *Polygon Lasso* can be used to enclose areas bounded by straight lines.

The Magic Wand tool bases selections on the color of objects.

Each of these tools features a set of controls (accessed on the *Tool Options* bar and via menu options) that make object selection simpler.

The selection tools are common to all Photoshop versions, with the sole exception of the *Magnetic Lasso* option, which is not offered in ImageReady.

The Marquee

We've already seen the *Marquee* in its secondary role as an alternative crop tool. In its default setting, the *Marquee* draws rectangular (or square) selections over an image, when dragged from one corner to the diagonal opposite. Once the selection has been made, the boundary is shown by a moving dotted line. Once the selection has been made you can crop it (as we have seen already) or copy it to the clipboard for use elsewhere. Using the *Cut* command will, like the similar command in a . wordprocessing program, copy the selection to the clipboard and delete it from the original image.

1|2|3 *The* Marquee *can be used to select elements from within an image. By using the selection tools (see right), compound selections (sometimes called 'Boolean') can be made, which comprise disparate marquee selections or connected (overlapping) selections.*

Inverting and Switching a Selection

The Selection Menu contains four commands for manipulating any selection.

– Choosing *Select > **All*** will select the entire image area (or, if parts of the image have already been deleted, all the remaining elements)

– *Deselect* removes all selections from the image.

– *Reselect* (obviously) reselects all the regions previously made inactive by the *Deselect* command.

– *Inverse* inverts the selection. All the selected areas become deselected and the deselected areas are selected.

Making compound selections

From Version 6 of Photoshop upwards, the creation of compound (multiple) selections has become much easier. Using any of the *Boolean* tools you can add to a selection (*Shift > **Select***), subtract an area from a selection (*Option > **Select***), and even use the area where selections intersect (*Shift > **Option***). Compound shapes involving, for example, rectangular marquees, circular marquees, and lassoed elements can be achieved easily. Subtracting the central areas from selections can also form shapes such as frames and annuli. The best way to discover the potential is to play with the tools on a copy of your image.

4 *The menu command* Select > **Inverse** *reverses the selected and deselected components of an image, useful as here for "framing" an object.*

5 *Frame selections are possible using the* Boolean *selection buttons.*

72 Feathering

It is appropriate at this point to introduce an essential feature that can be used with all the principal selection tools: *Feather*. When you make selections, your goal might be to apply an effect to it, or to use the selection as one component in a photo-montage. In either case, the result could appear very artificial. The selection boundary—which you will have precisely defined with one or other of the selection tools—may be too abrupt. In other words, it will appear "cut out," because the edges of the selection will be too sharp and make your sleight of hand very obvious. Feathering the edge of your selection gives you the opportunity to soften them and make them appear more natural.

Photoshop gives you two ways of applying a feathered edge. The first is in the *Tool Options* bar, and you can use it prior to making your selection. Using this option, you set a feather radius (measured in pixels) in the *Feather* box.

But to apply a feathered edge *after* making a selection, you can use the menu option *Select > Feather* and enter a feather radius in the dialog box. This is a useful fallback for those situations when, at the end of making a complex selection, you realize you've forgotten to set a feather radius.

In the illustrations here, the same selection has been made, but in each case a different feather radius has been set.

1

2

1|2 *The use of feathering to improve the blend of one image with another is shown in these images, using a radius of 10 pixels and 30 pixels respectively.*

3 *This tiger has been selected using the* Magnetic Lasso *tool with the feather radius set to 0 pixels.*

4 *If this is cut and pasted into a new image it has the characteristic "cutout" look, with sharp edges that are not sympathetic to the subject.*

5 *By altering the feather radius to only 2 pixels a softer edge is formed. Do this by either selecting the subject again with a feather radius specified, or by using the retrospective* Select > **Feather**.

6 *When this image is placed over a background (in this case a rough texture produced by the* Texture *filter) it blends in seamlessly.*

3

4

5

6

Creating a vignette

Although the idea of a vignette is a century and a half older than digital photography, its principles form the basis of many digital effects. In particular, it is used extensively in webpages today to create soft-edged images.

So, let's put the Victorian vignette aside and create something much more contemporary and pertinent to Web design.

❶ Select an image to use as a basis for the vignette. It's a good idea to choose one that is not too tightly cropped in on the subject.

Select the *Rectangular Marquee* tool. Set a feather radius of, say, 25 pixels. The most effective radius will depend on the image size and resolution; you may need to alter this figure later for a better result.

❷ Start the *Marquee* selection from a point inside one corner and drag to the opposite corner. When you release the mouse button, the rectangular selection you have drawn will change to a round-cornered rectangle to account for the feather radius.

Invert the selection (*Select > Inverse*). This makes the border around the area selected by the *Marquee* the active area.

❸ Press the *Delete* key to create the vignette. The border is deleted to reveal the background color complete with a graduated transition to the image.

❹❺ Although vignettes were traditionally either rectangular or oval in form, there is no reason to stick to convention. You can just as easily create a vignette using irregular forms, as we've shown here.

74 Selections based on color

The *Marquee*—as an "overall" selection tool—
is limited in its ability to make selections based on
rectangular, oval, or irregular forms. Apart from its
application in making frames or vignettes, this tool
is rarely appropriate for most types of manipulation,
where your intended selection area is likely to be
irregular. The *Magic Wand* tool, on the other hand,
gives you the opportunity to make such selections
by using color as the criteria. If you have an object
that is predominantly one color, the *Magic Wand*
can pick it up.

To use the *Magic Wand* you need to click within
the intended selection area. All the adjacent pixels
that match the color of the one that you have
clicked on will be appended to your selection. At
such a simplistic level of usage, the results are
unsatisfactory since color variations and fluctuations
mean that many adjacent pixels do not precisely
match. That's why the tool features a *Tolerance*
setting. Once you set a tolerance (of between 0
and 255) any pixels whose color falls within the
tonal tolerance range will be selected. By judicious
setting it then becomes easy (either all at once or
by making multiple selections) to select your object.

TIP

Grow and Similar

Sometimes you'll find the *Magic Wand* selection
"misses" some pixels (particularly at the edge of the
selection and sometimes within) because they fall
just outside the tolerance range. Use the *Grow*
command (*Select > **Grow***) to append these to the
selection. To append pixels of similar color to your
selection that are not contiguous with the selection
use the Similar command (*Select > **Similar***). A
typical use would be when selecting the sky in an
image. By using *Similar* all those pieces of sky
visible through trees and foliage, for example, can
be appended to the selection.

❶ Let's look at how we can use the *Magic Wand* to change the color of this star fruit from yellow to blue.

❷ Select the *Magic Wand* and set a tolerance of 32. (This is the default value and a good median value to use.)

Click on an intermediate colored part of the image. (For clarity here, we've colored the selected area each time.)

❸ With a tolerance of 60 you will get a better selection.

❹ Don't set the tolerance any higher than this. If it is set to 80 it will begin to draw in elements of the surroundings!

❺ Instead, add to the selection by using the *Boolean Add to Selection* button on the *Tool Options* bar.

❻ By making multiple selections, using the more modest tolerance, you will be able to select the whole object.

Note that to change the color of the object use the *Hue/Saturation* command to change the hue. This preserves the detail in the selection. Using a paint tool would simply flood the selection with color.

❹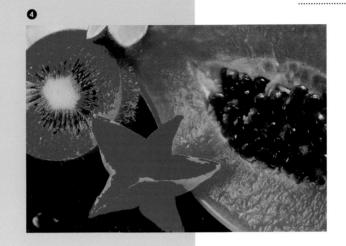

❺

❻

Color range command

A relative of the Magic Wand is the *Color Range* command (*Select* > **Color Range**, in Photoshop only). You can use *Color Range* to select a color in the original image to form the basis of your selection and, by altering the *Fuzziness* (another name for tolerance), alter the amount of similar tone that is included in the selection. You can monitor the selection in a preview box.

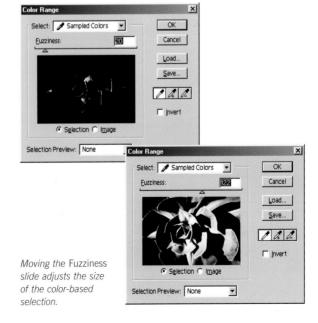

Moving the Fuzziness *slide adjusts the size of the color-based selection.*

76 The Lasso

We've been saving the best—or perhaps the most useful—of the main selection tools until last. This is the tool that lets you make freehand selections. Whether you want to cut a person from a scene or select an object to paste elsewhere, this is the ideal solution. In fact, in the more recent versions of Photoshop, the *Lasso* has become a trio of tools, with the original freehand selector being joined by the *Magnetic Lasso* and the *Polygonal Lasso*.

The *Magnetic Lasso* automatically detects an object boundary and follows it. It is not foolproof—it will, in cluttered scenes, occasionally follow the wrong edge—but on the whole it makes accurate selection a great deal easier.

The *Polygonal Lasso* creates straight-sided selections. By clicking from corner to corner, or point to point, a selection boundary is created. It works best on subjects that are broadly rectilinear.

Specify an edge detection width (you can specify any number between 0 and 40 pixels). This determines how close an edge needs to be from the mouse pointer to be detected. Where there is the chance of alternate edges being detected and followed it is wise to set a low figure.

Edge Contrast determines how sensitive the *Lasso* will be to edges. Enter a percentage figure here. The *Lasso* will only detect prominent, high-contrast edges when a high value is set. If the edge contrast is low, set a lower number.

Frequency specifies the number of fixing points (i.e. the number of fixed attachments to the detected edge) that are laid down. A high value anchors the selection border more securely and faster. More moderate values are appropriate where the edge has lower contrast since this will prevent firm attachment to the wrong edge.

Quick masks

Quick Mask boasts a well-deserved place on the Photoshop toolbar (though sadly not in Photoshop Elements) and is a great way of both creating and modifying selections. When using the *Quick Mask* you are not restricted by the conventional selection tools but can use any painting tool to add or remove areas from a selection.

When you switch to Quick Mask mode, your image will be overlaid by a transparent red layer. If you have previously made a selection that area will be clear. Now you can take a paintbrush, for example, and by selecting white as the paint color, paint additional areas onto your selection. The mask disappears from these areas. Conversely, by selecting black as the paint color you can add to the masked areas.

The efficacy of the Mask is probably best demonstrated by using it for real.

1

TIP

The original quick mask

The *Quick Mask* imitates the Rubylith—a red, ultraviolet light-opaque compound that is painted onto printing plates to prevent that part of the plate from being affected by the photogravure processes. Unlike the Rubylith, you can change the *Quick Mask* color: doubleclick on the *Quick Mask* toolbar button and then click on the color window. Shift-clicking while in *Quick Mask* creates straight lines.

1 *For most practical selection purposes the* Magnetic Lasso *is the most appropriate tool to use. To get the best from it you'll need to set the parameters in the* Tool Options *bar.*

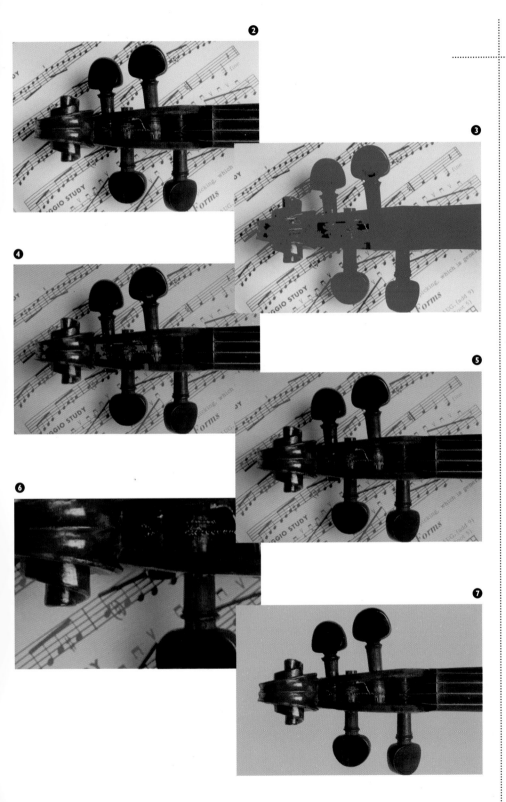

❷❸ Begin by making a selection using any of the selection tools. On this occasion —and just on this occasion!— absolute accuracy is not required. Here multiple use of the *Magic Wand* has succeeded in selecting most of the subject (a violin) but some parts have been missed and others (the music notation, for example) appended. Blue has been used to show the extent of the selection here.

❹ Press the *Quick Mask* button on the toolbar. The characteristic red mask is applied to areas not selected.

❺ Begin by removing mask from the violin. Select white as the paint color from the toolbar and pick a small paintbrush. Paint over the mask areas. If, due to heavy-handedness, you remove too much mask don't worry. You can correct this later.

❻ Switch the paint color to black and begin adding masking to the areas outside the violin that have been inadvertently picked up by the *Magic Wand*. (You can also correct any mistakes made when you removed the mask.)

❼ Select *Normal Mode* to convert the mask to a selection. Then invert the selection and press delete to reveal the background color.

⁷⁸ PAINTING TOOLS

Image-editing applications' ancestry can be traced back to the basic painting applications such as Microsoft's Windows 1 accessory MS Paint. They were designed for simple graphics and, to a degree, also to demonstrate the capabilities of the emerging graphical user interfaces (GUIs).

The painting tools that made their debut in these early days still have a place in the toolbox of today's applications such as Photoshop. These include: *Paintbrush, Clone/Rubber Stamp*, and *Pencil*. In this same category are the more specialized tools such as *Art History Brush, Gradient*, and *Line Tool*.

- The **Paintbrush** creates soft strokes of color with, depending on the brush size and type selected, soft or firm edges. The brush size can range from a single pixel through to a space-filling 999 pixels.
- For some the *raison d'etre* of digital imaging, the **Rubber Stamp** tool uses existing image elements —rather than simple paint color—to paint with. As such it is has a rather different application to the simple painting tools, although details of brushes and usage are similar.
- The **Pencil** tool creates hard-edged lines.
- The **Airbrush** option on the Tool Options bar introduces airbrush-like dynamics to the Paintbrush tool. Press to toggle on or off. With this selected you can select any brush tip and use it to lay down a continuous stream of paint. Build-up continues even when the cursor is held still.

TIP

Straight up

Painting tools offer casual freehand painting options. Where you need to draw a straight line with the *Pencil* or *Paintbrush* click on the starting point of the line then, without dragging, click on the endpoint while holding down the *Shift* key. Use this to fade the size, color or, pressure of your brushstrokes.

Painting tools require subtle application if their effect is not to become obvious. This also applies (perhaps to a lesser extent) to the *Rubber Stamp* tool—careful use of it can blend cloned areas seamlessly with an image's original pixels.

Brushes

To use the *Paintbrush* tool (along with tools like the *Rubber Stamp*) you need to select a brush size first. The painting processes on a virtual canvas are much like it is in the physical world: sometimes you'll need a large brush suitable for filling large areas of canvas, sometimes a fine one suitable for detailing. In Photoshop you can also create your own or customize an existing one should you have specialist requirements.

1

1 Using a paint tool alone for image manipulation can lead to artificial-looking results.

2 Photoshop provides a large palette of default brushes from the fine to the coarse. This set also includes some "spatter" and "diffuse" brushes.

If you need more than this then you've got a couple of options. The simplest is to click on the Palette Options button (the small arrowhead to the top right of the palette). The popup menu that appears offers several sets of brushes (including Calligraphic, Faux Finish *and* Natural) *which can be appended to your palette.*

2

3

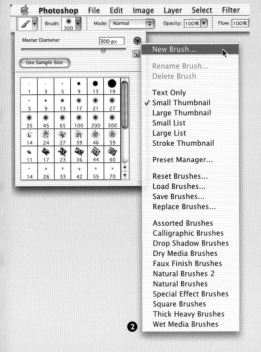

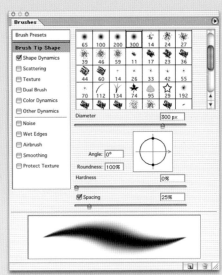

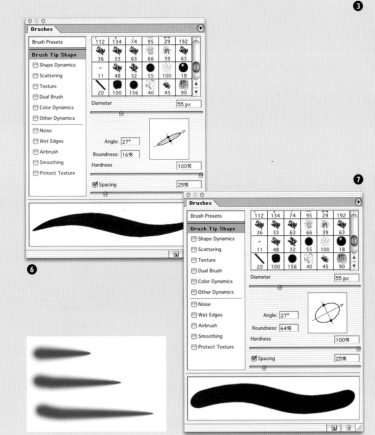

Creating a new brush

❶ For a simple brush select a brush head type and master diameter from the *Brushes* dropdown menu. Click on the right arrowhead to open the pop-out menu to save and name your chosen brush.

❷ To create a bespoke brush open the *Brushes* palette (drag it from the *Palette Well* or select *Window > Brushes*).

❸ To base the brush on an existing one, select the appropriate brush type to set the fundamental characteristics.

❹ You can select *Airbrush* or *Wet Edges* (for example) to give the brush the characteristics of an airbrush or a laden watercolour brush, respectively.

❺ To alter the spacing of brush applications (in the range 1% to 1000%) select *Brush Presets* and then *Spacing*. Clicking on *Shape Dynamics* permits additional control over the brush's roundness and randomness ("jitter").

❻ Alter the shape of the brush head using the window (push or pull the axes of the ellipse) or enter angle and roundness settings in the appropriate box.

❼ Note that the settings are echoed in the live preview box on the palette. Save your brush.

Brush dynamics

Click on the small button on the *Tool Options* bar to display (and change) the brush presets. Here you can alter the "fadeout" of the brush in terms of its size, opacity, and color.

80 **The Art History Brush**

The *Art History Brush* shares a menu position with the *History Brush*. Click on this to display the popout menu then select *Art History Brush*. In Photoshop Elements this brush effect is offered by the *Impressionist Brush*, and has its own toolbar position. Photoshop 7, meanwhile, comes with an *Impressionist Brush*, along with others in its Art History Brush Presets. In Photoshop you need to set a *History State* for your source image data.

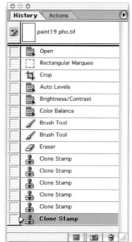

① Open the *History Palette* (if it is not already on the desktop). This shows a sequential history of all the manipulations you have applied to the image.

Click in the left column of the state you want to use as the source for the tool.

Select the *Art History Brush* tool and a brush size.

② Select an option from the *Style* menu to paint with.

Enter a *Fidelity* amount. This determines how much your colors will vary from those of the original. Lower numbers mean greater deviation.

Enter an *Area* value. This represents the area covered by your paint strokes, with larger values giving greater coverage and more numerous strokes.

③④ Paint across the image. Here are some typical results.

TIP

Why Art History means smaller files

Using the *Art History* brush doesn't just create a painterly image—it can help create more compact files when you come to optimize them. Because of the way in which the image is broken into strokes it is easier to compress and you can even reduce the number of colors. (We'll explore file optimizing in the next chapter.)

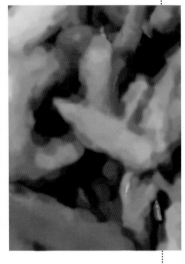

The Impressionist Brush

Although more modest in its attributes, the *Impressionist Brush* can be used to make photographic images resemble paintings. Take care to select a brush size that is appropriate for the image, and beware of overusing the effect and erasing the original image's components. Don't reduce the image to meaningless blocks of color.

Like the *Art History Brush*, the *Impressionist Brush* features a set of control parameters that can be used to set the brush size, the extent of the effect, and the painting type. The latter parameter can be set to tight strokes (short, long, or medium), more informal, loose strokes, and a series of curled strokes. Each provides a noticeably different effect. As you can see from the examples here, the degree of "impressionism" (art history snobs beware!) imparted by each varies significantly. The *Tight Long* stroke setting gives this view of Montmartre and the Sacré Coeur in Paris an Impressionist look, which the painters who occupy the slopes there might just admire. The *Loose Curl* obscures much of the original and creates a far more abstract effect.

1 *The* Impressionist Brush *has been used here with a modest brush setting and a style setting of* Tight Long *(strokes).*

2 Impressionist Brush *style set to* Tight Long *strokes.*

3 Impressionist Brush *style set to* Loose Curl *strokes.*

Gradient tools

Gradient tools are particularly useful for
Web graphics. Use them to create subtle
(or not-so-subtle) color gradients as
backgrounds or fills.

To create a basic gradient drag the
cursor from a start point to an end point.
A soft, color gradient is created with
the current foreground color at the start
point and the background color at the
end point.

1|2 *A short distance
between start and end
points gives a steep
gradient, a longer one
(which may begin outside
the image or selection) a
noticeably softer one.*

3|4|5|6 *As well as the
simple* Linear Gradient,
*other options can be
selected from the* Tool
Options *bar.*

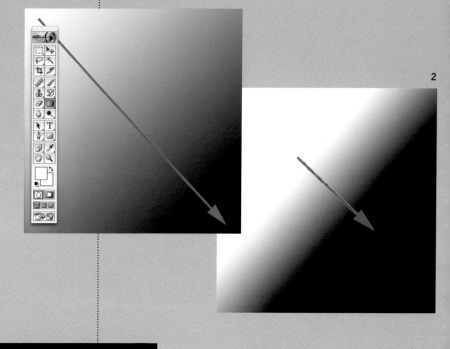

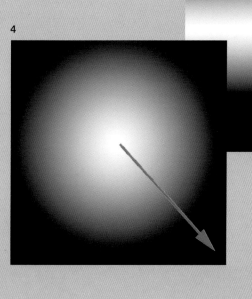

1 *Image background*

2 *Image Layer ("Paint Layer")*

Blending Modes

In many parts of Photoshop you'll come across *Blending Modes* options. Selecting a blending mode will determine how, for example, the pixels of an image background will interact with the layer above it or with any paint that is applied to it.

In some cases the effect is quite obvious. The *Dissolve* mode dissolves one layer into another, while *Color* uses only the color of the applied paint or layer to tint the background (this is a useful mode when tinting black-and-white images).

Below are the effects of Photoshop *Blend Modes* on two images (see the originals, *left*).

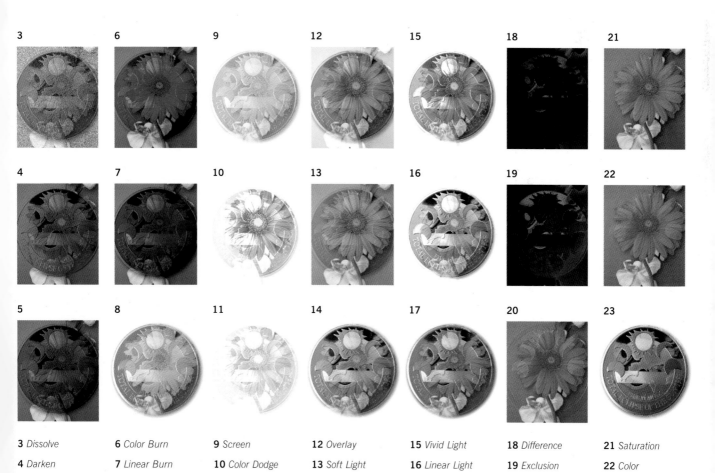

3 *Dissolve*	**6** *Color Burn*	**9** *Screen*	**12** *Overlay*	**15** *Vivid Light*	**18** *Difference*	**21** *Saturation*
4 *Darken*	**7** *Linear Burn*	**10** *Color Dodge*	**13** *Soft Light*	**16** *Linear Light*	**19** *Exclusion*	**22** *Color*
5 *Multiply*	**8** *Lighten*	**11** *Linear Dodge*	**14** *Hard Light*	**17** *Pin Light*	**20** *Hue*	**23** *Luminosity*

84   Cloning with the Rubber Stamp tool

If there is a tool that, to the average user, characterizes digital image manipulation the clone tool is it. Called *Rubber Stamp* by Adobe, this is the most potent of manipulation devices. It differs from other tools in that it does not use paint to obscure underlying objects, but pattern and texture from another part of the image. Equally, it can be used to paint objects in from another part of that image, or from another image entirely. Uses include:

- Removing "street furniture" from landscapes. You can clone adjacent areas of an image to obscure road signs, TV antennas and dishes.
- Moving elements. Adding or removing people from wedding photographs is one example, as is 'opening' the eyes of a subject who blinked.
- Cleaning up a scene, where dust, scratches and other blemishes spoil the image.

Heal and Patch tools

The *Heal* and *Patch* tools debut in Photoshop 7. Both permit the copying of one part of an image to another, but are more subtle and less 'destructive' than the *Rubber Stamp* can be. The *Heal* tool is designed for working with small areas, while for larger areas the *Patch* tool is more effective. You can use any selection tool to select the area to be patched and then, by dragging the selection to an area for a source texture, the repair can be effected.

TIP

Stamp on it!

Remember when using the *Rubber Stamp* tool that it stamps new pixels over existing ones. When removing a road sign from a scene, for example, you should do so by painting over it with pixels from nearby that have a similar tonal range. To successfully remove an object, therefore, you need to have sufficient pixels from elsewhere in the image to clone from and stamp over the object. If the object is large, this might be a problem, but it might be possible to use another image as the "pixel donor".

1|2 *Unsightly artifacts need not compromise an image. A moment's work with the* Rubber Stamp *tool can restore the scene to a pristine state.*

1

2

❶

Stamping out unwanted artifacts

❶ This view would be much improved without the TV antenna and cabling. You can clone the sky around the antenna to paint over it.

Select the clone from a point in the foliage and move the mouse to part of the signage.

❷ Use the stamp tool to gently paint over the object. Because there is a risk that the eagle-eyed viewer might spot the cloning work here, change the point of the clone occasionally to create a more random pattern. (You can also alter the transparency in a similar way.)

❸ The finished effect is much cleaner.

❹ You can also clone objects into, or around, the scene. As a final whimsical touch we cloned a copy of the downstairs window into the eaves of the house using exactly the same process.

❷

❸

❹

86 Sharpening and softening

There can be few tools in image manipulation that are as abused and misunderstood as the *Blur* and *Sharpen* effect filters. There is a strong belief that the *Sharpen* filter is a cure-all for those images that are not critically sharp. This, sadly, is not true.

To understand the *Sharpen* filter you need to understand the mechanics that underpin it. All this filter actually does is identify areas of change in an image; for example, where there is a change in the contrast of the tone. After identifying these gradients it makes the transition steeper. The result is a perceived increase in sharpness within the image. The crucial factor is that sharpening does not add any detail to an image. It is, after all, impossible to restore to an image detail that was not present in the first place.

Unsharp Mask

Photoshop does, however, provide (among several sharpening filters) the *Unsharp Mask* (USM) filter that, when properly used, can improve the perceived sharpness and quality of an image.

The subtleties of unsharp masking are such that whole chapters of books—if not complete books—could be written about it, but for our purposes a more modest set of criteria need be analyzed.

The *Unsharp Mask* filter emulates a traditional technique wherein a photographic film negative is sandwiched with a slightly unsharp positive when printing. The result is increased edge sharpness determined by the degree of "unsharpness" in the positive (a similar technique is used in the reprographic industry in the printing process).

Three parameters define the sharpening characteristics possible with the *Unsharp Mask* and these are shown in its dialog box: *Amount, Radius*, and *Threshold*.

Amount determines the degree of sharpening applied. The higher this figure the greater the amount of sharpening.

Radius defines the number of pixels over which sharpening will take place. Entering an amount here of, say, three pixels tells Photoshop to look three pixels from an edge when evaluating sharpening.

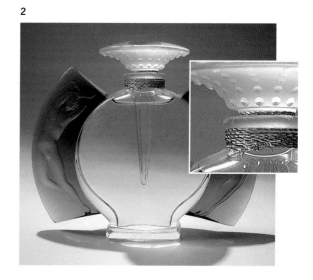

1 *Amount 0, Radius 0, Threshold 0.*

2 *Amount 250, Radius 1, Threshold 0.*

3

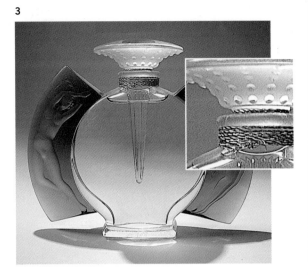

4

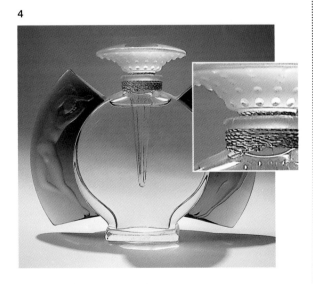

Setting a *Threshold* sets a minimum contrast level for sharpening to be applied. Pixels with levels below this will be unaffected by any changes.

To explain the complex interplay between these parameters it is best to describe two sharpening situations. In the first we want to sharpen an image but don't want to sharpen the finest details. This fine detail is referred to as "high frequency" detail. A typical example would be a flattering portrait. We want to make the eyes, hair, and mouth as sharp as possible but don't want to sharpen every detail (and blemish) of the skin.

Low versus high frequency detail

The second situation is when we need to retain and sharpen this high frequency detail but the lower frequency is less significant. One example of this situation might be a townscape where the overall shape of the landscape (the buildings, low-frequency detail) is sufficiently defined already but the detailing—such as windows, tile, or brickwork —needs to be sharpened.

For the portrait we might make settings of *Amount* 75 percent, *Radius* 5, and *Threshold* 5. The townscape would have settings of *Amount* 150 percent, *Radius* 1, and *Threshold* 0. These should, however, be regarded as starting figures. It is best with this filter to monitor the effect directly on the image and continue to make minor adjustments until the desired effect has been achieved.

In this set of images we've applied the parameter settings as indicated. Be aware of how large-scale and small-scale detail changes with the different settings. Don't overdo the sharpening, even when using unsharp masking. With the radius raised to ten pixels the effect is obvious and unpleasant artifacts are introduced.

3 *Amount 250, Radius 3, Threshold 0.*

4 *Amount 350, Radius 1, Threshold 25.*

88   IMAGE FIXES

We've seen many of Photoshop's manipulation and fixing tools, so let's take a look at a few practical cases so you can get a feel for how they work.

The PhotoCD image

If you use PhotoCD images (whether of your own artwork or as supplied by picture libraries) this might be typical of the image quality you receive. On superficial inspection it seems fine, but a closer look reveals it to be slightly unsharp and the levels are poorly distributed. Add to this a poor frame and this definitely needs improving!

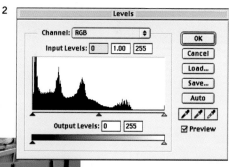

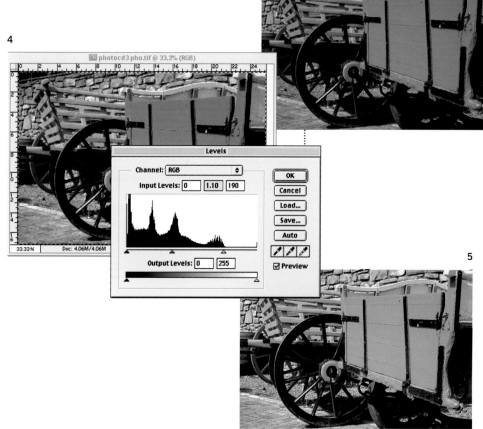

1 *Our original PhotoCD image: good, but could be better.*

2 *The* Levels *dialog shows that it sadly lacks in some quarters.*

3 *Address the poor frame by using the crop tool to trim the dark borders. Irrelevant areas like this need to be cropped prior to any adjustments to* Levels. *Otherwise the black border will be taken into account when making level assessments.*

4 *Adjust the levels by dragging the right-hand slider to the right-most group of pixels. (A deficiency in this area is often characteristic of a PhotoCD originated image.)*

5 *Next use the* Unsharp Mask *filter to restore a little sharpness to the image. PhotoCD images do tend to be recorded a little soft. Use modest settings of 100 percent for* Amount, *2 for* Radius, *and 0 for* Threshold.

❶

❷

❸

❹

❺

Soft-focus portrait

Creating a soft-focus effect is not the same as blurring a sharp image, as we've already mentioned. The aim when creating a soft focus image is to retain virtually all the detail in the original,then to give an overall soft, diffused glow. Here's a simple way of achieving this effect.

❶ Open your image and perform any other edits first. (The application of soft focus should be the final stage.) Create a duplicate layer based on this image (*Layer > Duplicate Layer*).

❷ Apply a *Gaussian Blur* (*Filters > Blur > Gaussian Blur*) to the layer. A modest amount of blur (say five pixels) is usually sufficient. You obviously need to blur the image while not losing too much of the detail.

❸ With the layer active adjust the transparency slider on the *Layers* palette. Monitor the effect directly on the image. (A transparency of between 40 and 60 percent is normally adequate.)

❹ Save the image (save in Photoshop format if you want to preserve the layers). Note how the detail of the original is retained but soft halos surround the highlights and there is an appealing softness across the image, rather than a blur.

❺ If we compare close-ups of the softened image (left) with one given a similar degree of blur (right) the difference is all too obvious.

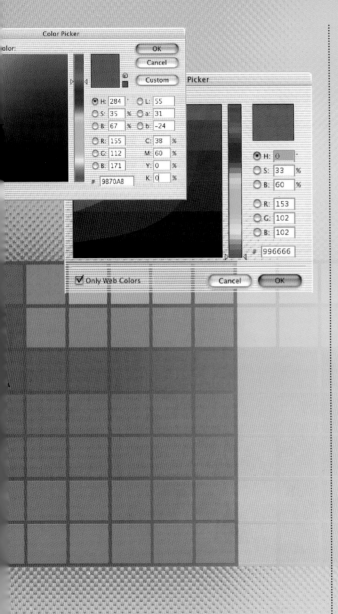

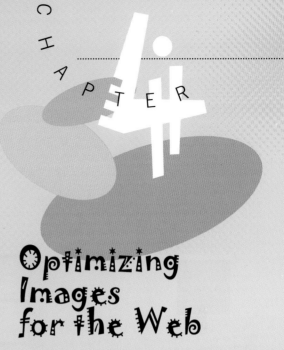

Optimizing Images for the Web

Whether they contain graphics or images, Web files need to be saved in Web-savvy formats. The three principal ones (as we've already discussed) are GIFs, JPEGs, and PNGs. The final selection from among these three will be determined by the type of visual and, to a lesser extent, the use to which it will be put. Let us look more closely at the options and analyze the distinctions more closely. But first, why do we need to optimize our images in one of these formats?

92 THE OPTIMIZING BALANCING ACT

There's a fine line to tread when it comes to creating graphics for the Web. On the one hand you should aim for the highest quality. No doubt a great deal of effort will have gone into your artwork, and you won't want it to be compromised. But to deliver it in an efficient way that doesn't leave website visitors fuming as they wait minutes for the download is a challenge. This leaves Web designers in a seemingly insoluble quandary: high-quality image, or small file size?

The solution must be for you to find the optimum tradeoff between quality and size. It is partly to balance these conflicting demands that the three file formats exist and, although it looks as if the three are vying for your attention, that is rarely the case. Each has, in all but a handful of cases, well-defined strengths that make it a champion for a particular type of file.

The optimized file

What distinguishes an optimized file from its larger progenitor? It is partly the characteristics of the format in which it is saved, but more significantly it is the size of the file. This is the crucial feature that permits an apparently large file to be delivered effectively over the Web. Each of the principal formats uses some form of compression, and as a result compromises the image to a greater or lesser degree. It is always advisable to edit your image using a more robust format (such as the Photoshop-native PSD format) that retains both the quality and the features (such as layers) of the original image. Only when you are happy with your image do you need to optimize it. Don't discard the original image either! Chances are you will want to return to it later and refine or alter the image in some way. This is much easier and will deliver better quality if done on the original rather than on the optimized copy.

The Web file formats

Here's a summary of the main Web file formats, indicating their respective strengths and weaknesses.

JPEG (Joint Photographics Expert Group)

- Supports 24-bit color (16.7 million colors).
- Ideal for continuous and graduated tone images (i.e. photographs).
- Can support high compression ratios.
- Quality deteriorates with increased compression.
- Handles high-contrast images (or areas of flat color within images or graphics) poorly due to the compression technique.
- Liable to show compression artifacts.
- Artifacts are cumulative with successive opening and saving of a file.
- The most common form of distributing and delivering photographic images over the Web.

1

2

Best used for

1 Photographic images.

2 Large files needing heavy compression (at the expense of quality).

3 Graphics featuring gradients.

Welcom

GIF (Graphics Interchange Format)

- Uses a Color Table (an index of all the colors within the image) that is stored as part of the image data.
- Allows a maximum of only 256 colors in an image file.
- Better suited (as a rule) to graphic images rather than photographs.
- Permits transparency (only when one of the colors is defined as transparent).
- Effective at compressing images, particularly on graphics with large areas of solid color.
- Supports animation (the only one of the three formats to support this).
- Can contain all the 216 Web-safe colors (Mac and PC share 216 out of the 256-color palette).
- Dithering is often required to create intermediate colors not in the Color Table.

Best used for

Vector graphics (including type-based graphics).

Graphics with transparency.

Animations.

PNG (Portable Network Graphics)

- Features two variants: PNG-8 and PNG-24. PNG-8 is similar to GIF (but does not offer animation); PNG-24 is similar to JPEG but supports multiple levels of transparency
- Not supported by the rapidly decreasing number of older browsers.
- Should only be used if you know the recipient's browser supports it.
- Not as well supported by other proprietary image-editing and graphics applications.
- A less harsh compression regime results in (usually) larger compressed files.

Best used for

Vector graphics.

Graphics with gradients and transitions.

1 *Type featuring type effects (such as glows and drop shadows).*

2 *Graphics with transparency (PNG-8) or multiple levels of transparency (PNG-24).*

1

2

94 CREATING OPTIMIZED IMAGES

Now you are more familiar with the Web image formats and what they can (and can't) do, let's look at how to create an optimized image.

Previewing optimization

It is crucial to be able to preview the optimized result before any final commitment is made—bearing in mind that when optimizing a file you could compromise the quality beyond an acceptable limit. Photoshop, ImageReady, and Photoshop Elements all offer the opportunity to view optimization settings as they are applied to an image and give you the chance to compare these settings with your original image.

1 In Photoshop select *File > Save for Web* to display the *Save for Web* Dialog. Then select either the *2-up* (the original and one optimized) or *4-up* (original and three different optimizations) display mode. Optimizing settings are shown to the top right of the images, with the color table below.

2 In ImageReady you need only click on the appropriate tab (*Optimized, 2-up* or *4-up*) below the image title bar for a similar multi-image display. Optimizing information and the color table are displayed in their respective palettes.

1

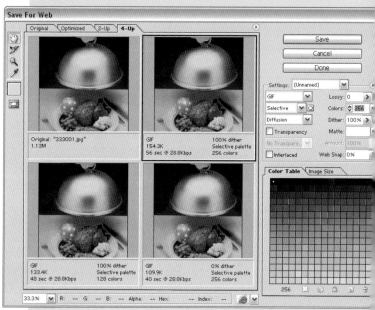

2

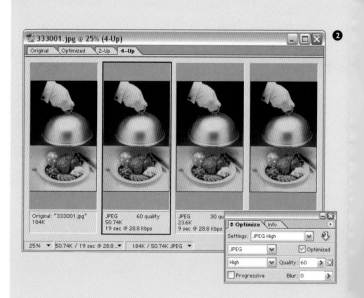

TIP

Engineering a smaller file

You might be wondering if you can create a smaller file size without compressing too far? If you are designing a graphic or editing/choosing an image then yes, you can.

To get a smaller JPEG, look for images that feature gradients, rather than contrasty edges. By the same token, softer images (not necessarily blurred) can be more effectively compressed. If you can lower the contrast too, you'll make some modest gains.

For a more compact GIF, design your graphic with large areas of flat color and avoid colored gradients. Choose a smaller number of colors (but reduce the amount of dithering).

Setting the optimization for an image

Let's use Photoshop's *Save for Web* option to create an optimized image. We could, equally, use the ImageReady equivalent, but sticking with Photoshop makes description much simpler.

If you are unfamiliar with the practicalities of file optimizing, select different settings and observe the results on the image (zooming in where necessary for a closer look).

❶ In Photoshop the *Save for Web* option assumes you have an image already open. If you don't, open the appropriate image now.

Select *Edit > Save for Web* to open the dialog box. The currently active image will appear in the window.

Note the tabs across the top of the window. *Original* will display the original, non-optimized image. *Optimized* displays only the optimized image configured as in the Settings box to the top right. The *2-up* and *4-up* displays compare the original with one or three optimized images.

❷ Select *2-up*. In a few moments you'll see an optimized image appear in the right-hand pane of the split screen. Click on that image and you'll see a highlight frame appear and the *Settings* box will display the appropriate settings used to optimize the image.

❸ You can use the *Hand* and *Magnifying Glass* tools to examine the image more closely. The title box below the optimized image displays not only the details of the image, but also advises about the compressed file size and roughly how long it would take to download this file using a connection of the speed shown.

❹ You can select a modem speed by clicking on the arrowhead above the image and choosing your preferred option.

❺ Select an alternative optimization from the pulldown *Settings* menu, which offers a range of presets (*GIF Dithered* and *No Dither*, *JPEG*, and *PNG*) or make specific selections from the options in the box beneath.

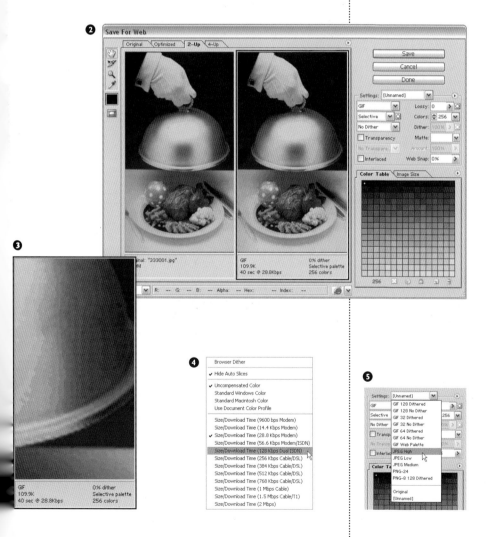

96 The Optimize palette controls

ImageReady's *Optimize* palette (and the equivalent pane in the *Save for Web* dialog) is context-sensitive and displays settings appropriate to the regime selected from the *Settings* pull-down menu.

Optimizing a photograph

Apart from some exceptions already outlined, photographs will need to be optimized using the JPEG format. This process can be conducted in Photoshop or ImageReady.

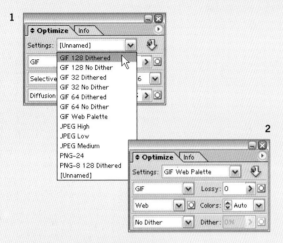

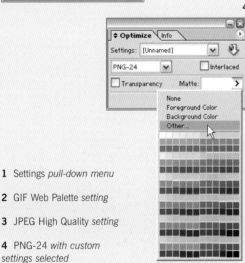

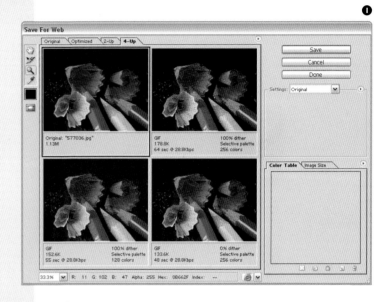

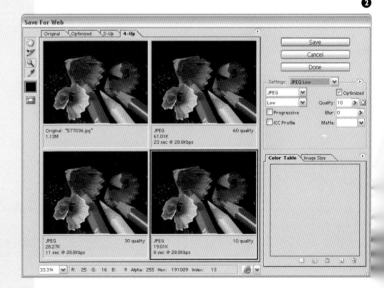

1 Settings *pull-down menu*

2 GIF Web Palette *setting*

3 JPEG High Quality *setting*

4 PNG-24 *with custom settings selected*

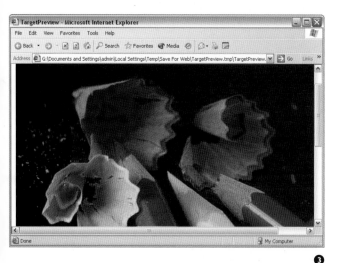

3

Optimizing an image to a target size

Both Photoshop and ImageReady give you the option of compressing an image file to a precise, predefined size. Called the target size, this process puts the onus of compression back into the hands of the host application.

In Photoshop open the image you want to reduce to the target size. Open the Save for Web dialog box.

6 Select *Optimize to File Size* from the pullout menu to open the dialog box

7 Enter the required file size in the box. You can choose whether to base the optimization on the current settings in the *Settings* panel or allow ImageReady to automatically select between GIF or JPEG regimes to get the best result.

Click *OK*. The new file size and quality details will be displayed.

In ImageReady you should use a similar method but select *Optimize to File Size* from the *Optimize* palette menu.

Open the image to be optimized.

1 Choose *File* > *Save for Web* (in Photoshop), or click the *4-up* tab on the open image and ensure the *Optimize* palette is visible (in ImageReady).

2 Choose JPEG as the file optimizing format (if a color table was visible earlier it will now disappear; as color tables only relate to GIF images). We have selected the three JPEG presets available from the drop-down menu for this example.

3 Click on the icon at the base of the screen to preview the image in a browser.

You can now make changes to the quality. Try reducing the quality in stages and observing the results.

4 5 Turn the *Progressive* option on or off. With *Progressive* off (unchecked) the image downloads piecewise from the top (baseline mode). With *Progressive* on, the whole image downloads immediately at low resolution then progressive downloads follow at higher resolution.

4

5

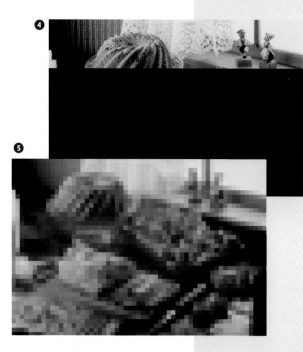

Baseline (top) and Progressive (above) JPEG images at equivalent stages of download.

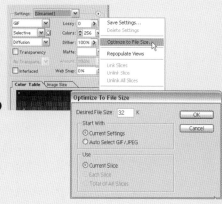

6

7

98   Selective JPEG compression

The process of selective JPEG compression works on the premise that a typical image contains some areas—the principal subject for example—that are more important than others. It is effective on large images (and less so on smaller ones where the additional instructional information may actually increase file sizes).

This process uses the Photoshop feature known as the *Alpha Channel*. Normally this channel, which is in addition to the standard red, green, and blue channels in an image, contains information relating to the transparency of the image, and acts as a mask. Here it will be used to indicate areas of the image to which different degrees of compression should be applied.

❶

❷

❶ Open your image and assess which elements are the most significant. In this picture of a flower you should preserve as much detail as possible on the bloom.

❷ Use a selection tool to select the bloom. Of those explored in the last chapter, the *Magic Wand, Lasso*, and even *Quick Mask* would be effective here.

❸ Choose *Select* > **Save Selection**. You'll be prompted to give the channel a name.

Display the *Channels* palette to see the new *Alpha Channel*. Invert the channel by choosing *Image* > *Adjustments* > **Invert**.

Without closing the image open the *Save for Web* dialog box and click on the circle icon next to the *Quality* box.

❹ Choose the new *Alpha Channel* and in the *Modify Quality Settings* dialog adjust the maximum and minimum quality settings.

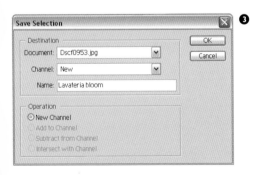
❸

❹

JPEG2000: the best of both worlds?

Although JPEG is the standard for image compression on the Web, it is a flawed format. Compression losses and artifacts make it very much the selection of necessity rather than choice. JPEG2000 is a more recently devised format that promises to offer a solution.

Developed by the Berlin-based LuraTech it uses wavelet technology to overcome the blocky artifacts normally associated with JPEG. It also allows both lossy and lossless compression in a single image file. Here's an image section that has been compressed at a ratio of around 1:100 with JPEG and JPEG2000. While the technicalities of the format are outside the scope of this book, it is clear from the illustrations here that the promise of good compression and preserved quality is being kept.

JPEG

JPEG2000

100 **Optimizing a graphic**

The process for optimizing a graphic is very similar to that for optimizing a photographic image, with the obvious exception of GIF being the preferred file format. Some of the adjustments you need to make, however, are quite different. Let's walk through the process and look more closely at the differences using the logo of the Aurina Group.

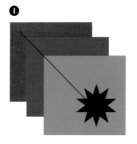

❶ ❷ With the image open, select *Save for Web* (in Photoshop) or click on the *4-up* tab (in ImageReady). Note that this time, because you are using a GIF, the *Color* table is populated with colors from the image.

Select GIF as the file format in the *Settings* panel or the *Optimize* palette.

❷
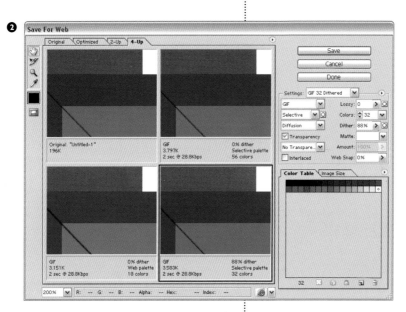

❸ By selecting *Browser Dither* (from the popout menu above the top left menu) you can see how the colors, not all of which are Web-safe, might be dithered on an 8-bit monitor.

❹ Select a *Color Reduction* algorithm. You can monitor the changes in the image windows. Here is what the graphic looks like with the *Web* option. (See our Tips on the bottom left of this page for an explanation of the *Color Reduction Algorithms*.) Also select a *Dither* algorithm (*Noise, Pattern,* or *Diffusion*).

Adjust the number of colors, bearing in mind that fewer colors give smaller files but could compromise quality.

Select a *Lossy* setting (making this high compacts the file size but it can compromise quality) and *Web Snap* setting. Use this to snap colors to the nearest *Web-safe* color. Higher percentages will result in more colors being snapped to their nearest equivalent.

Once the settings have been made (and you've had a chance to preview the results in a browser), save the image.

TIP

Color reduction algorithms

Because all GIFs are restricted to a maximum of 256 colors you'll need to determine which colors end up in the color table. The color reduction algorithms save you much of the effort and compile the table for you. There are four options.

Adaptive works by sampling colors from the spectrum that appear most commonly in the image. You can reduce the number of colors in the color table to seemingly unfeasible levels (say 30) but still get very acceptable results.

Selective is the default setting in Photoshop and ImageReady. It works by giving greater importance to areas of continuous color and also tries, where possible, to preserve Web colors.

Perceptual biases its selection toward those colors to which the human eye has greater sensitivity.

Web restricts the colors to the 216 Web-safe colors described previously.

❸
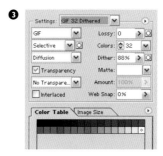

❹
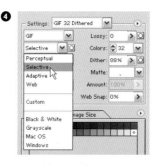

Selective Compression of GIF files

As we employed selective compression for JPEG files, so we can with GIF files. We can use channels again to effect this and modify (either singly or in combination) the *Dither* amount, *Lossy* compression level, or *Color Reduction* algorithm.

❶

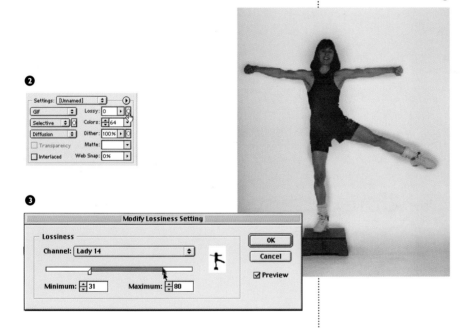

❷

❸

❺

❹

❶ Begin by making a selection around the most significant or important parts of the image. (This can be one region or, using the *Boolean* selection tools, several disparate ones.) Alternatively you can use Photoshop's *Quick Mask* mode and paint the mask over the areas that you wish to maintain.

Make this selection into an Alpha channel by choosing *Select > Save Selection* and giving the channel a name.

❷ Select the small icon next to the *Lossy* compression window in the dialog box (*Save for Web* dialog in Photoshop, *Optimize* palette in ImageReady.) Choose the channel you have just saved.

❸ As with the JPEG selective compression, choose maximum and minimum compression settings.

❹ Alter the dither amount in the same way, selecting the small icon adjacent to the *Dither* setting window.

❺ After you have made changes to the compression in this way, check the image as a whole to ensure that its integrity has not been compromised, as it has been here. It is possible sometimes to compress less important areas of an image to such a degree that the boundaries become prominent.

102 EXPLORING WEB COLOR

Whatever graphics application you choose, the resultant files will be in a specific color mode. When your goal is an image to print from your desktop inkjet printer, the choice of color mode isn't crucial, but for the Web, RGB (Red, Green, Blue) is the mode you will ultimately have to work with. Having RGB Color as the default mode in your image editing program is actually quite useful. In fact, ImageReady can only create or handle files in RGB mode. This is due to all computer monitors (on which the work will be displayed) featuring red, green, and blue phosphors for image reproduction. Where you are creating a new image it is wise to work entirely in RGB Color mode to prevent the color shifts that are (to a greater or lesser degree) inevitable when mode changes are made.

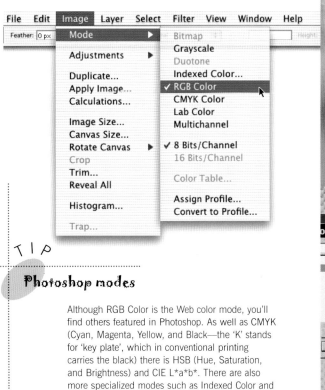

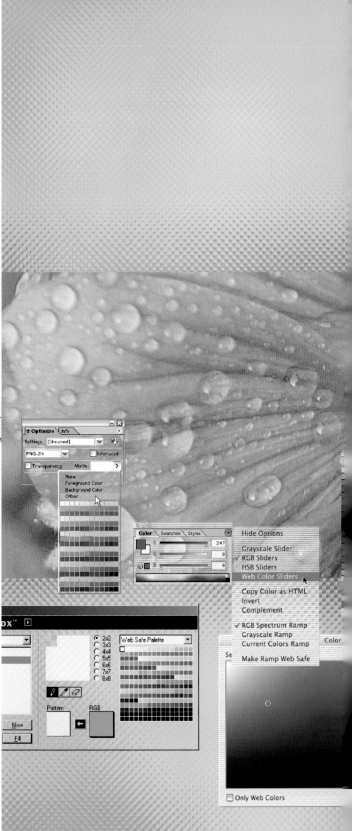

TIP

Photoshop modes

Although RGB Color is the Web color mode, you'll find others featured in Photoshop. As well as CMYK (Cyan, Magenta, Yellow, and Black—the 'K' stands for 'key plate', which in conventional printing carries the black) there is HSB (Hue, Saturation, and Brightness) and CIE L*a*b*. There are also more specialized modes such as Indexed Color and Duotone. These are fully explained in Photoshop's online Help.

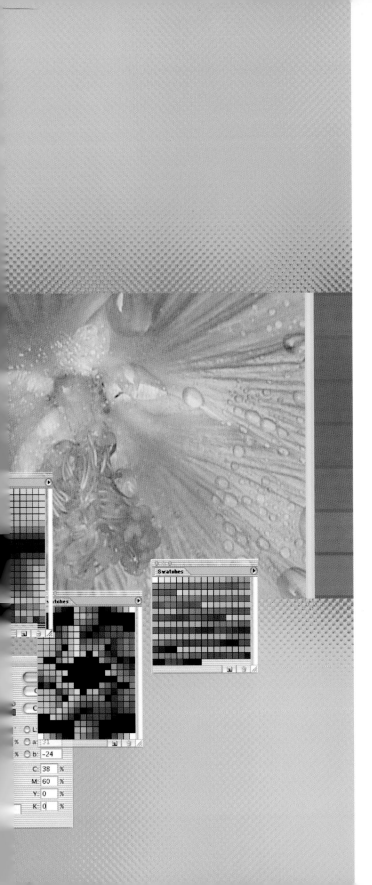

Web color palettes

The problematic nature of working with colors on webpages arises, as we mentioned much earlier, from the countless display options (monitors) available to those who might access your work via the Web. Different browsers, color adjustments, and most importantly, color bit-depths abound, and risk compromising compatibility.

In order to reduce the risks to an acceptable level, a color palette was devised that could be used to create images that could be successfully viewed on all computer systems. Hence we have the Web-safe color palette, whose colors are common to both Macintosh and PC platforms.

Origins of Web-safe colors

Web-safe colors were introduced in 1994 by Netscape to address a problem with graphics operating systems that had been exacerbated by the appearance of Web browsers. At that time, most computers could only display 256 colors and these 256 colors were not standardized across applications and webpages. This had the inevitable consequence that, when two pages—each with its own set of 256 colors—were displayed on the same screen the result was chromatic chaos.

With the aim of introducing order into this chaos, Netscape introduced their definitive set of 216 colors evenly distributed through the RGB palette. When a webpage adopted this color set (as virtually all did) pages would look okay.

Web-safe swatches

It is much easier to work with Web-safe colors if you have them loaded into your Swatches palette. Use the Load Swatches command from the Swatches palette menu to add them to your swatch selection. You'll be asked whether you want to replace the current selection or append to it.

104   The Color Picker and Color Table

The *Color Picker* displays all the colors that can be selected and used in your image or, by clicking the *Only Web Colors* button, just the Web colors.

1 *The* Color Picker *in Photoshop enables color selection either by selecting a tone from the panel (after first making a broader color choice from the vertical color bar), or by entering absolute values in the boxes. You can enter values corresponding to colors in either the RGB, CMYK, HSB, or Lab color models.*

2 *With* Only Web Colors *selected, the more limited range of colors is displayed. The display can be altered by selecting one of the radio buttons (here brightness, B, has been selected).*

3|4 *In keeping with the RGB mode-only nature of ImageReady, there is a more limited range of direct entry options in ImageReady's* Color Picker. *Alternate displays are again possible by selecting different radio buttons. (Here we have chosen* Hue *and* Green.*)*

The Color Table *palette displays, in the same manner as the* Color Swatches *palette, the colors present in a GIF or PNG-8 image. You can use the table to add or delete colors, snap a color (convert to the nearest Web-safe color), and lock colors (to prevent changes).*

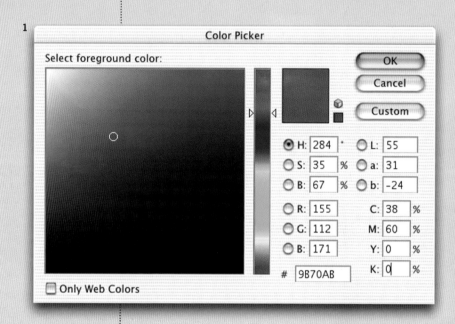

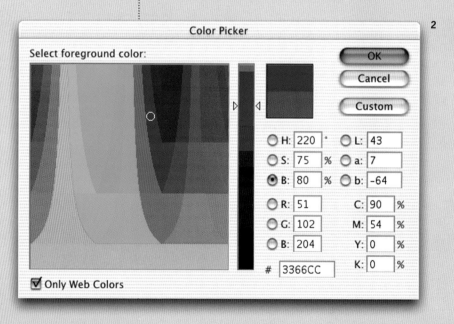

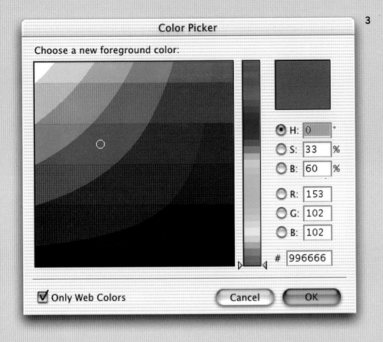

3

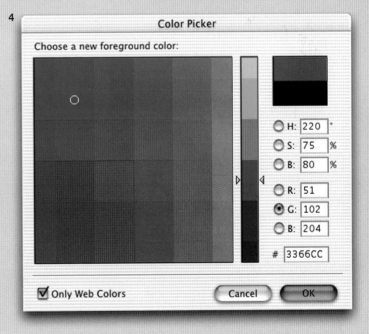

4

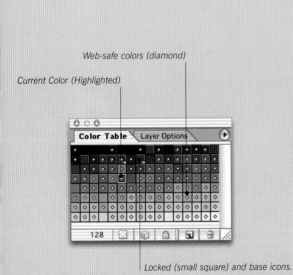

Current Color (Highlighted)

Web-safe colors (diamond)

Locked (small square) and base icons.

106

Choosing and using Web-safe colors

Web-safe colors can be chosen using the *Color Picker*, the *Color* palette, or by using the *Swatches* palette (Photoshop, Photoshop Elements, ImageReady). Let's look first at *Swatches*.

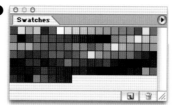

❶ Display, or open the *Swatches* palette (*Window > Show Swatches*). Here the default set is loaded.

Click on the arrowhead to open the pop-out menu.

❷ Select one of the Web-safe swatch sets. *Visibone, Visibone2, Web Hues, Web Safe Colors*, and *Web Spectrum* are all equally valid selections.

❸❹❺❻❼ To avoid the possibility of confusion, it's a good idea not to append these colors to the existing swatches. You can always reset your default selection later by selecting *Reset Swatches* from the pop-out menu.

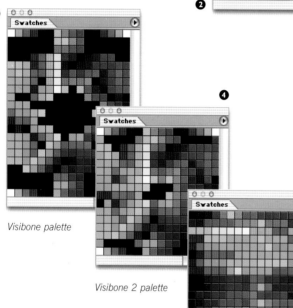

Dock to Palette Well

New Swatch...

✓ Small Thumbnail
Small List

Preset Manager...

Reset Swatches...
Load Swatches...
Save Swatches...
Replace Swatches...

ANPA Colors
DIC Color Guide
FOCOLTONE Colors
HKS E
HKS K
HKS N
HKS Z
Mac OS
PANTONE metallic coated
PANTONE pastel coated
PANTONE pastel uncoated
PANTONE process coated
PANTONE solid coated
PANTONE solid matte
PANTONE solid to process
PANTONE solid uncoated
TOYO Colors
TRUMATCH Colors
VisiBone
VisiBone2
Web Hues
Web Safe Colors
Web Spectrum
Windows

Visibone palette

Visibone 2 palette

Web Hues palette

TIP

The hexadecimal code

Each Web-safe color is given a unique "name" using hexadecimal (base 16) notation. Six hexadecimal numbers denote Web-safe colors. The first pair defines the amount of red in the image; the next two the amount of green; and the last two the blue. Conventional hexadecimal numbers use the numerals 0 to 9 along with A, B, C, D, E, and F, but for Web-safe colors only 0, 3, 6, 9, C, and F are used and these are given in pairs: 00, 33, 66, 99, CC, and FF, limiting the number of possibilities for each color to six, and the number of combinations to 6 x 6 x 6 or 216.

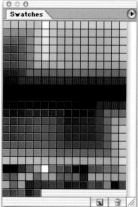

Web Spectrum palette

Web-Safe palette

Using the
Color Picker

Click on the foreground (or background) color in the toolbox to open the *Color Picker*.

1 Click on the *Only Web Colors* box to restrict the display to Web colors only.

2 Choose a color. Note that the "normal" continuous color display has been broken into a limited number of tones—each of which is a Web-safe color.

You can also choose a Web-safe color directly from the all-colors *Color Picker*.

3 Open the *Color Picker* again but ensure that *Only Web Colors* is unchecked.

Select a color from anywhere on the color pane.

Click on the "cube" icon adjacent to the before/after color selection to change the color to the nearest Web-safe color.

Note that once a Web-safe color has been selected the cube icon will disappear. The icon will not appear if the color selected manually is Web-safe.

☑ **Only Web Colors** **1**

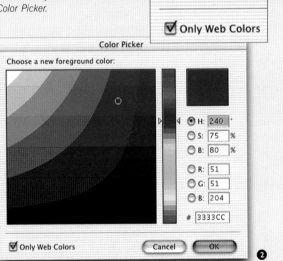

2

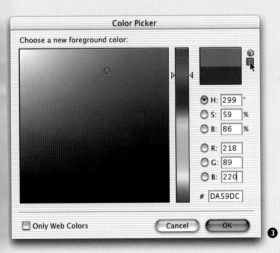

3

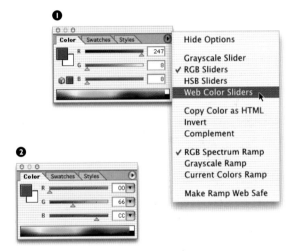

x

Using the
Color Palette

Open (or select) the *Color* palette.

1 In the pull-out menu select *Web Color Sliders*.

2 Adjust the sliders. Note that, although they look like conventional sliders, each can only be moved to one of six pre-set positions.

Also note the alphanumeric displays to the right of each slider. This is the hexadecimal value (see box) for the color selected, in this case 0066CC. This number is also displayed (or can be entered) in the space (indicated with a #) at the bottom right of the *Color Picker*.

108 THE DITHERBOX

What happens when you want to use a precise
color—such as matching a corporate color—but
the Web-safe palette doesn't feature it? Rather
than accept a close alternative (which may not
be close enough!), you can use Photoshop's
DitherBox to simulate it (not available in
Photoshop 7). As the name suggests, it uses
dithering processes to mimic the new shade,
but in this case it is you that decides
the dithered color and how it is constructed.

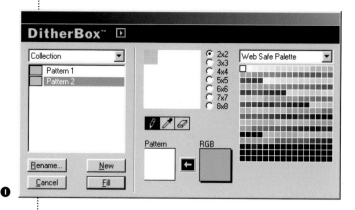

❶

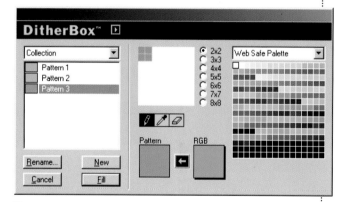

❷

Creating a new shade

Begin by selecting the non-
Web-safe color that you wish
to copy. If you have *Web Color
Sliders* active you'll need to
select an alternative, otherwise
you'll be restricted to the Web-
safe choices.

❶ Open the *DitherBox*. Select
*Filter > Other > **DitherBox*** to
display the DitherBox dialog
box. This features a central
mixing palette (where colors
can be mixed), a set of Web-
safe colors, and a list of any
dithered colors you may have
already created, grouped into
"collections".

❷ Note that your selected color
appears in the RGB swatch box
below center. Click on the arrow
to its left and a pattern of Web-
safe colors that are equivalent
to your chosen color will appear
in the left-hand box.

You can now give this new
color a name and save it as
part of your collection.

You can select a new color from
the *Color Picker* by clicking on
the RGB color swatch. Then
click on the arrow to see the
dithered equivalent of this.

❸ When you come to use the
dithered colors you can click on
the right-facing arrowhead in
the title bar to collapse the
dialog box so that only the color
collection is shown.

❸

TIP

Sending images across the Web

When you need to send images across the Web
as an email attachment or as a download from a
website (rather than an element within a webpage)
you don't have to be quite so concerned with colors
and color regimes. An image delivered in this way
can be in full color and need not be restricted to
the Web file formats (though because of their
smaller size you may choose to use such formats).
You need only ensure that the file can be opened
once it is on the recipient's computer.

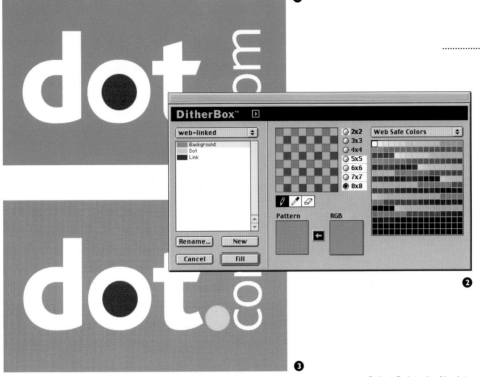

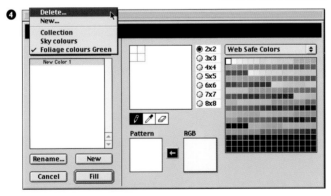

Select Delete (or New) to
delete or add a collection.

New collections of colors
are easily created and
named for future reference.

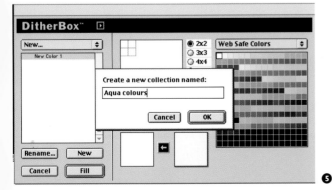

Applying your new shade

You can apply your newly created shade by clicking on the *Fill* button in the main (left-hand) pane of the *DitherBox* dialog window. The *DitherBox* dialog box closes after the fill has been applied.

Applying a saved dither pattern to a new image

Once a dither pattern has been saved it can be applied to any image.

① Open the image to which you wish to apply the dither. Use the selection tools to select an area of the image you wish to fill with the pattern.

② Select the *DitherBox* filter (*Filter > Other > DitherBox*). Choose the collection that contains the pattern by clicking on the *Collection* popup menu

③ Click *Fill*. The dither pattern is applied and the dialog closes.

Editing dither patterns

If you have an extensive collection of dither patterns you can use the following editing routines to manage and rearrange your collection.

⑤ Create a new collection. Click on the *New* button (at the top of the collections popup menu. Give the collection a name and click OK.

Delete a *Collection*. Select the collection as before and click on the *Delete* button.

⑥ Rename a collection. Select the collection using the *Collections* popup menu. Click on the *Rename* button.

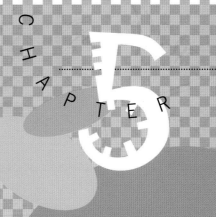

C H A P T E R

More Advanced Image Manipulations

Whether your aim is to manipulate images that will only be delivered over the Web, or to create enriched graphics for a website, we've already seen that Photoshop offers a host of tools to improve your source material. Now let's investigate some more of Photoshop's manipulation tools.

112 FILTER EFFECTS

Although the name was derived from the lens-mounted photographic filters used to enhance exposures in-camera, Photoshop's digital effects filters are capable of a whole lot more. The filters fall into distinct categories that you will find listed under Photoshop's (and ImageReady's) Filters menu. Many of these are illustrated in detail in this chapter, but to give a feel for each category here is a rundown of what you can expect from each.

Artistic filters

Filters in this group provide painterly and artwork-style effects. *Colored Pencil* and *Dry Brush*, for example, give your image the appearance of having been created using these media tools, while *Cutout* simulates a paper collage effect.

Blur filters

These are designed to introduce different types of and varying degrees of blur. A typical use for the *Blur* and *Blur More* filters is to increase the depth of field in a scene. The more controllable *Gaussian Blur* can be used to introduce controlled softness into a layer. *Motion Blur* and *Radial Blur* create "grabbed" movement effects by blurring in specific directions.

Smart Blur is another controllable blurring tool. Set a blur radius (indicates which pixels are to be included in the blur), a threshold level (below which pixels will not be included in the blur), and a blur quality, and you have incredible control over the eventual amount of blur.

1

2

1|2 *Artistic filters can make an image appear as if it were created in an artist's medium. This is shown by the* Colored Pencil *and* Rough Pastels *here.*

3

Brush Strokes filters

Although arguably a subset of *Artistic* filters, the *Brush Strokes* set contains a wide variety of brush- and ink-stroke effects. With these there is a particular emphasis on revealing texture in the applied strokes.

Distort filters

From a subtle wave pattern through to three-dimensional transformations, the small set of distortion filters actually offer a large range of powerful effects. Some—like *Diffuse Glow* —are more artistic in their approach but others perform complex, and, in Adobe's own words, "memory hungry" image distortions.

Noise filters

The Noise filter set offers opportunities to both add noise to an image and remove noise and similar artifacts. *Despeckle* is a useful filter that will remove random noise (and even some dithering) to give a slightly softer image. It is a useful filter to apply prior to using JPEG compression as the lessening of edge contrast can lead to more effective compressions (the mild softness introduced is barely noticeable). A more extreme version, *Dust & Scratches*, can come to the rescue of dirty or mishandled scanned prints. It removes small blemishes across the image (or selection) at the expense of overall sharpness.

   Add Noise introduces noise (rather in the manner of a film grain pattern), which can be useful for softening gradients that have been created with limited color palettes.

Pixelate filters

In some form or another all the filters in this group exaggerate the pixel structure of the image by grouping pixels in larger "clumps", which are then given an average color value.

3 Motion Blur *is ideal for giving static objects a sense of motion.*

4 Radial Blur *(Zoom mode) creates the impression of zooming during exposure.*

5 Radial Blur *(Spin mode) gives a strong rotational motion effect.*

4

5

114 Render filters

Here's the solution if you need to create your own skyscape background, want to add lens flare to a shot, or change the existing lighting pattern. The *Lighting Effects* "filter" is actually a large portfolio of effects that can alter the lighting balance in a photo or add dramatic (and obvious) additional lights.

Sharpen filters

Sharpen filters were first mentioned on page 86 [Section 3]. If you use either the *Sharpen* or *Sharpen More* filters (the latter has around four times the effect of the former) you will only increase the *perceived* sharpness in an image, not the actual sharpness or detail. Remember too that sharpening an image can make the image file larger when it is compressed using JPEG, and can also make the JPEG image artifacts more obvious.

Once you are familiar with the fiddly *Unsharp Mask* filter (see page 86), you'll probably have little time for any other *Sharpen* filters.

Sketch filters

The *Sketch* group is another set that should really be part of the Artistic group. It is an eclectic mix of filters since only some of them create the effect of sketching media. Others give new textures to images. Perhaps characterizing the differences between using Photoshop for "pure" image editing and using it as a means to produce Web graphics,

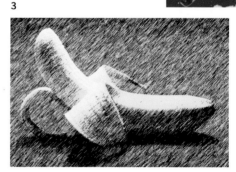

TIP

Elements' filter palette

Stealing a march on its elder sibling, Photoshop Elements features a *Filters* palette that displays thumbnails of each filter, which are listed alphabetically. You can drag and drop a filter onto your image or selection to apply it. Alternatively, you can doubleclick on a filter, adjust the settings, and then click *Apply*. You can also choose to display just the filters from one category by selecting that category from the dropdown menu.

Elements' Filters palette

1 Lens Flare *is an example of a* Render *filter.*

2 Sharpen *filters increase the perceived, not the actual, sharpness.*

3 *Like* Artistic *filters,* Sketch *filters give painterly or artwork-style effects.*

4 Stylize *filters include* Extrude, *here.*

5 Texture *filters such as* Craquelure *give impart deep textures to images.*

6 Tile Maker *is an easy way to produce tiled back-grounds for webpages.*

4

5

6

Tile Maker

● Blend Edges   OK

Width: 10 percent
☑ Resize Tile to Fill Image
○ Kaleidoscope Tile   Cancel

filters of the latter type (including *Note Paper, Plaster, Stamp*, and *Torn Edges*) rarely find photographic application but are useful for producing graphic shapes from an image and forming webpage backgrounds or graphic designs.

Stylize filters

The *Stylize* filters come into their own when creating innovative graphics for the Web or print media. However, when used "straight" they are so identifiable in their effect that they will be easily recognized by your peers, who may find the look more invidious than individual!

Texture filters

These can create textured images (in a similar way to the photographic darkroom texture screens that were popular in the 1970s). The group also features some pseudo-pixelation effects that are good for converting continuous tone images to graphic forms. These can be converted into GIFs later.

Video filters

The two *Video* filters *De-interlace* and *NTSC Colors* are concerned with improving the quality of a TV-sourced image (in the case of the former) and converting an image to match the color space of NTSC format television (in the latter).

Other filters

This category is home to the *DitherBox* (see page 108) and other filters with either specialized or indeterminate effect. Also included is a *High Pass* filter (to remove low-frequency detail) and *Maximum* and *Minimum* filters (for modifying image masks). ImageReady features a modified filter set in this category, which comprises *DitherBox*, *Offset*, and, uniquely, *Tile Maker*. This modifies an image or image selection to make it suitable for use as a tiled background in a webpage. Images can be flipped horizontally and vertically to create kaleidoscopic effects.

116 FILTER EFFECTS

A single image (**1**) can be turned into as many new pictures as you can imagine, by applying one of Photoshop's filter effects. Not all of the basic filter sets have names that allude to their true effect, however, so below and over the next few pages the results of applying various Photoshop filters to this original image are illustrated. Where appropriate, filters have been applied using the default settings and with black and white as foreground and background colors respectively.

Artistic filters

2 *Colored Pencil*

3 *Cutout*

4 *Dry Brush*

5 *Film Grain*

6 *Fresco*

7 *Neon Glow*

8 *Paint Daubs*

9 *Palette Knife*

10 *Plastic Wrap*

11 *Poster Edges*

12 *Rough Pastels*

13 *Smudge Stick*

14 *Sponge*

15 *Underpainting*

16 *Watercolor*

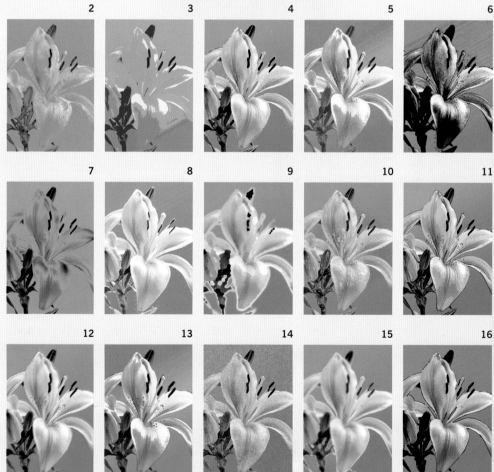

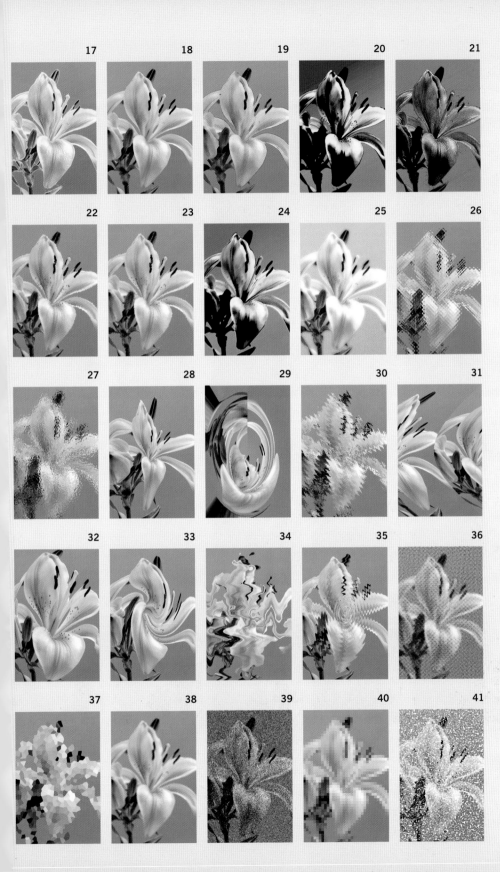

Brush Strokes filters

17 *Accented Edges*

18 *Angled Strokes*

19 *Crosshatch*

20 *Dark Strokes*

21 *Ink Outlines*

22 *Spatter*

23 *Sprayed Strokes*

24 *Sumi-e*

Distort filters

25 *Diffuse Glow*

26 *Glass*

27 *Ocean Ripple*

28 *Pinch*

29 *Polar Coordinates*

30 *Ripple*

31 *Shear*

32 *Spherize*

33 *Twirl*

34 *Wave*

35 *Zig Zag*

Pixelate filters

36 *Color Halftone*

37 *Crystallize*

38 *Fragment*

39 *Mezzotint*

40 *Mozaic*

41 *Pointillize*

2 3 4 5 6

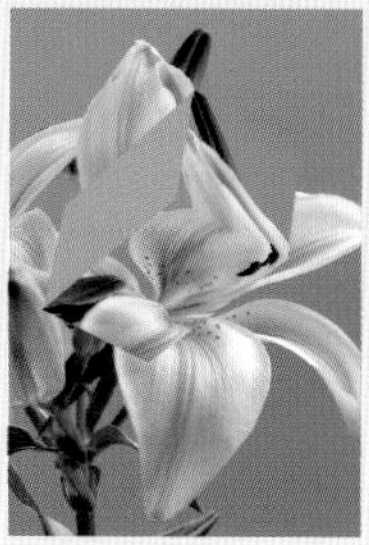

1

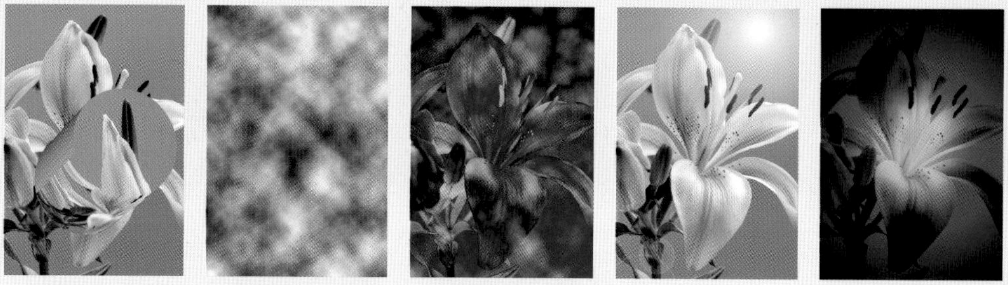

7 8 9 10 11

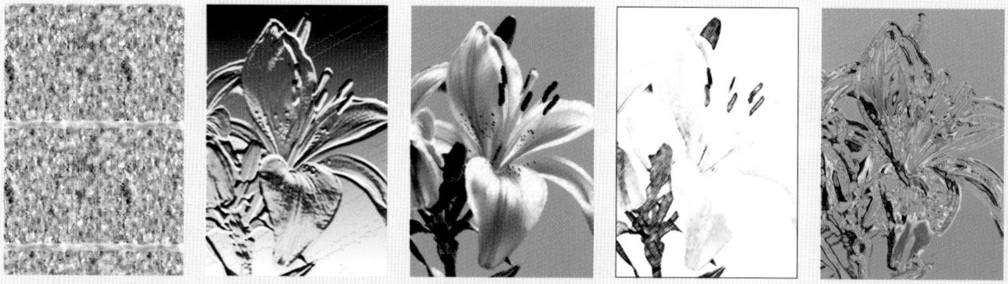

12 13 14 15 16

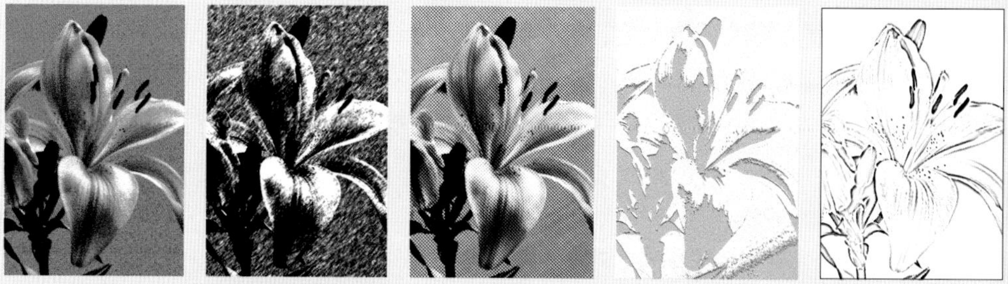

17 18 19 20 21

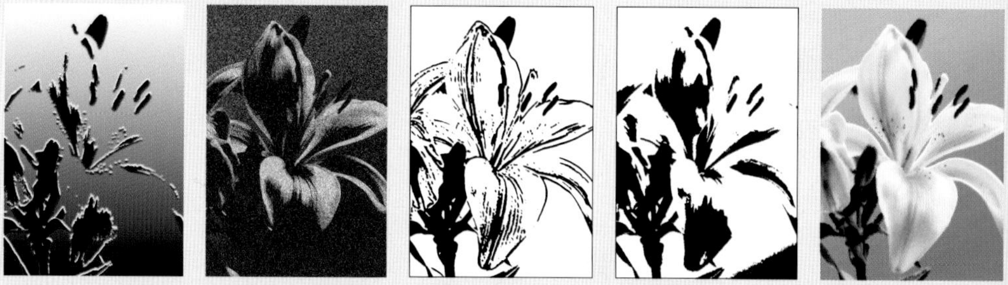

Render filters

1 *3D Transform, Cube*

2 *3D Transform, Cylinder*

3 *Clouds*

4 *Difference Clouds*

5 *Lens Flare*

6 *Lighting Effects ("Blue Omni")*

7 *Texture (Frosted Glass)*

Sketch filters

8 *Bas Relief*

9 *Chalk and Charcoal*

10 *Chalk*

11 *Chrome*

12 *Conte Crayon*

13 *Graphic Pen*

14 *Halftone Pattern (Dot)*

15 *Notepaper*

16 *Photocopy*

17 *Plaster*

18 *Reticulation*

19 *Stamp*

20 *Torn Edges*

21 *Water Paper*

Stylize filters

22 *Diffuse*

23 *Emboss*

24 *Extrude (Blocks)*

25 *Extrude (Pyramids)*

26 *Find Edges*

27 *Glowing Edges*

28 *Solarize*

29 *Tiles*

30 *Trace Contours*

31 *Wind ("Blast" setting)*

Texture filters

32 *Craquelure*

33 *Grain ("Enlarged" setting)*

34 *Mosaic Tiles*

35 *Patchwork*

36 *Stained Glass*

37 *Texturizer*

120 USING FILTERS

Filters are so diverse in effect and application that there is really no right and wrong way to use them. But you should always be critical of a filtered image: there's a fine line between a powerful and an awful image.

Creating an artwork from an image

Creating an artwork from an image is a good way to explore the way filters modify the pixels of an image. It can also deliver a painterly version of your original image.

TIP

Filter previews

Some filters only have a single setting: *Blur*, *Sharpen* and *Sharpen More* are examples of these. When you apply one, the effect happens immediately. Others, like the *Dry Brush* example shown on this page, have multiple settings that need to be set before the filter is applied.
In almost every case you can preview your settings either in the preview window or directly on the image. Note that once you have applied a filter that filter appears at the top of the *Filter* menu. Click on this to reapply the filter to your chosen image. When you select it from this position it will be applied directly, using your last settings.

❼

❽

❾ **❿** **⓫**

❶ Choose an image. Portraits and landscapes respond equally well to this treatment.

Select a filter. This exercise uses those from the *Artistic* or *Brush Strokes* submenus. Use the thumbnails on pages xx to xx to get a feel for the different effects possible. Here we've used the *Dry Brush*.

❷ Like many *Artistic* filters, the *Dry Brush* gives the user control over the digital brush that will be used to repaint the image. You can alter the brush size (smaller sizes give more detail), brush detail, and texture.

❸❹❺ Here are the results shown in the image preview of setting a small brush size, large brush size, and low brush detail.

❻ Use the image preview to adjust the image to get the preferred look. When you're happy apply the filter. Examine the result closely and, if necessary, undo the effect and repeat the process using new settings until you get what you're after.

❼ For more dramatic effects than those offered by the *Artistic* filters, try the groups *Render* and *Stylize*. Here we've taken a basic still life and applied a selection of filters.

❽ *Tiles* creates casually distributed blocks.

❾ *Crystallize* breaks the images into sharp-edged regions of similar color.

❿ *Patchwork* imitates the look of needlepoint tapestry.

⓫ *Stained Glass* breaks the image in a similar manner to *Crystallize* but gives each fragment a black border.

122 Cleaning up using Dust & Scratches

Some of your source images will, when digitized, show blemishes due to dust and scratches. The appropriately named *Dust & Scratches* filter can expunge these at a stroke. But this is also a useful filter to use to demonstrate that filters are not magic cure-alls for image defects. In many cases, the *Healing Brush* and *Patch* tools, both new to Photoshop 7, offer more effective means of repair.

T I P

Filter fading

You can fade the effect of a filter by using the *Fade* command in the *Edit* menu (located in the *Filter* menu in earlier Photoshop versions). If a filter effect is too extreme you can fade it by selecting *Fade*. Here *Palette Knife* is shown at 100 percent then faded to 50 percent.

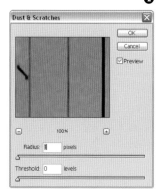

❸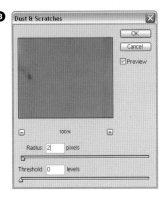

❹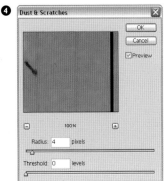

❺

❻

❶ Open your problem image. This one, due to bad care and (we assume) bad processing technique, suffers from both dust marks (particularly obvious in the sky area) and scratches.

❷ Select *Filters > Noise > Dust & Scratches* and this dialog will come up. Adjust the position of the image preview so that you can monitor the effect of any settings you make on the scratch marks.

❸ Set a radius and threshold. The radius is the distance (in pixels) over which you want dust and scratch marks removed. Think of this as a setting for the thickness of a scratch. In the threshold you can set a level below which you do not want marks removed. You might, for example just want them removed from a bright sky.

❹ Alter the radius. At the default setting of one pixel the finest marks disappear; increasing this to two removes both the finest lines and dust marks. Increasing it to four removes larger blemishes.

❺ However, the mechanism that removes blemishes also leads to a softening of the image. Setting the radius to six makes this more obvious.

❻ To get an effectively cleaned image you need to keep the overall radius low and select specific parts of the image that need to be cleaned more intensively. Apply an *Unsharp Mask* afterward to restore as much of the overall sharpness to the image as possible.

124 IMAGE PLUG-INS

One of the features that has given Photoshop its high standing is an underlying architecture that has been designed so that specific program extensions—known as plug-ins—can be added to provide extended functionality. Plug-ins can fit into a number of parts of the application (such as those for image acquisition and printing), but plug-in filters offer the greatest variety of options. By using your favorite Web browser and a search engine like Google, for example, you can probably turn up tens of thousands of these. Many are quite specific in their use and many more are, frankly, not worth downloading.

Useful sets are available both as Web downloads and commercial packages. Names to look out for include Eye Candy and Xenofex (both from Alien Skin Software), Paint Alchemy (Xaos Tools), and Andromeda. Most of the examples here are based on Eye Candy, mainly because it is so readily available.

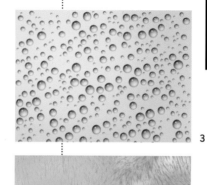

1

2

3

4

1|2 *Xenofex's Electrify plug-in filter sends bolts of lightning from the perimeter of a selection as it has done to this simple button.*

3|4 *Eye Candy's Water Drops give your images and graphics a very convincing sprinkling of water. If you've a fervent need for technicolor fur there's a filter for that too!*

5 *Once installed, plug-in filter sets appear in the Filter menu below the preset filter groups.*

6 *When additional plug-in sets are installed they appear at the base of the Filter menu and are opened in the same way.*

5

6

TIP

Portable plug-ins

Such has been the success of the filter plug-in concept that most of the premier image-editing applications also offer compatibility with Photoshop plug-ins. This gives you the advantage of being able to use many more plug-ins from other vendors. Should you need to use CorelDraw, for example, you can now take your favorite Photoshop filters with you. And, of course, use any CorelDraw favorites in Photoshop.

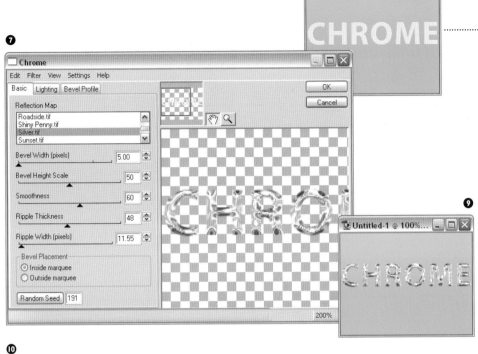

Using Eye Candy to enliven text

7 Create a new image with a plain or (as here) graduated background. Add some text.

8 Select a plug-in filter. We've used Eye Candy's *Chrome* for this exercise. You will need to monitor the results in the preview box very carefully.

9 Click on the tick (*OK*) to apply the effect to the image.

10 11 This time we've used the *Smoke* filter. The filter is applied over the selection (the text) and elsewhere. Plug-in filter effects are cumulative. If you repeat the effect (by clicking on the filter name when it appears at the top of the *Filter* menu) you can build up the intensity.

12 Apply the *Fire* filter to the text selection. Save the image as "Image 1".

13 Apply the filter again using the filter name at the top of the *Filter* menu. Save the image as "Image 2". Repeat this process another two times.

Now select the *Fire* filter from the Eye Candy menu but this time alter the filter settings to give a slightly different flame pattern. Apply and save the image.

14 Continue until you have around ten images. Each successive image will have a greater amount of flame.

126 EFFECTS

Currently exclusive to Photoshop Elements, the *Effects* feature is a great shortcut and lets you produce complex image effects by enacting a sequence of filters, layer styles, and even program functions automatically. Effects are displayed as thumbnails in the *Effects* palette. Toggle the display between full thumbnail and before/after thumbnails by clicking on the icons at the base of the palette.

For convenience, effects are grouped into categories:

Frames Creates frames and vignettes on an image or selection.

Textures Applies a texture to the image or selection.

Text Effects Applies compound effects to text layers.

Image Effects Compound image-based effects similar to some filter effects.

4

5

6

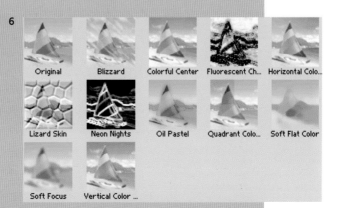

Applying an effect, selected from the palette, is very simple.

Open an image and, if you want to apply the effect to only part of the image, use the selection tools to select that area (otherwise the effect will be applied to the whole image).

Select the desired effect from the *Effects* palette then click *Apply*, or drag and drop the effect to the image or selection.

The effect is applied. As effects comprise multiple actions it may take a few seconds to complete.

Note that to undo an effect you will have to *Undo* or *Step Backward* several times to remove all the actions that have been individually applied to the image.

128 LAYER EFFECTS AND STYLES

If you're familiar with version Photoshop 5.5 or earlier you'll know all about *Layer Effects*. Rather like the effects described on the previous page, *Layer Effects* represent compound actions that are, in this case, layer-based. For reasons of rationalization, *Layer Effects* became *Layer Styles* from Photoshop 6 onwards, and with the launch of *Elements*. From here on we'll use 'layer style' to define both a single or compound set of actions.

You can add effects to most layers in Photoshop —the effects are added at the appropriate position in the *Layers* palette. You can also apply layer styles from the *Styles* palette in a similar way to adding effects in Elements.

Layer styles are most commonly applied to type to give it added prominence or an enriched texture. Styles such as *Drop Shadow, Inner Shadow* and *Glows* are frequently used to convert simple, flat text into something more substantial.

As you might expect, you can only apply layer styles to layers. The following examples will show you how to do this.

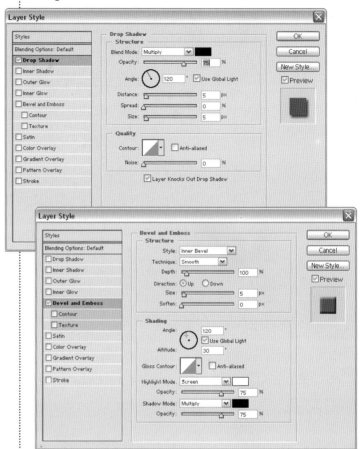

1 | 2 Layer Styles *dialog box for* Drop Shadow *(Win PC) and* Bevel and Emboss *(Mac).*

Layer styles and the Layer palette

You can add layer styles using the *Layers* palette. When you have entered your text in a type layer, click on the effect icon at the base of the *Layers* palette (indicated as a small "f" in a circle). The layer style options will appear as a dropdown menu. Select any to open the *Layer Styles* palette. In ImageReady you can also use the icon on the *Layers* palette. Clicking on a layer style will open the respective *Layer Style* palette (as demonstrated here, *right*).

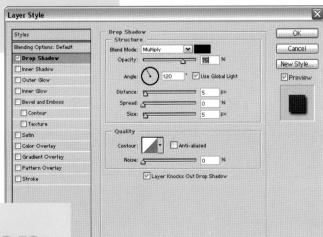

❶

Autumn Colors

❸

Autumn Colors

❷

Autumn Colors

Adding a drop shadow

Here's how to add the simplest of layer styles to a piece of text.

❶ Type your text onto your image. This will automatically create a type layer and enable you to use layer styles.

❷ Select *Layer > Layer Styles > Drop Shadow* to open the *Layer Styles* dialog box.

❸ You can use the dialog box to set the drop shadow parameters, for example the distance of the shadow from the layer objects (in this case the type), the lighting angle and the spread of the shadow. The small box to the right illustrates the effect of any changes you make. Apply the drop shadow.

❹ Note that you can also change the color of the drop shadow by clicking on the *Color Swatch*. This will open the *Color Picker*. Here is the same image with a purple shadow.

130 **More Layer Styles**

Once you've discovered how easy it is to add a drop shadow, you'll find that adding other layer styles is equally easy. Select the layer style from the menu (in the *Layers* palette or *Layers > Layer Style* menu). The parameters differ slightly on each but the method of application is the same.

Here are some more layer styles, applied to text:

Inner Glow gives slight relief to text. It is subtler than other 3D-effects, such as *Bevel and Emboss* (see below).

Inner Shadow gives type a "cut out" appearance that suggests you are looking through to a background.

Outer Glow is a useful effect for providing a visual separation between text and any background image.

The layer style *Bevel and Emboss* enables a range of effects that imparts a 3D feel to selections. When used with type this can often give the appearance of raised type (similar to that on a credit card), depressed type, and even rounded pillow effects.

TIP

Low-contrast colors

If the colors you must use on your website are very similar to one another or have low contrast, using a hard, tight drop shadow can give sufficient emphasis to make the colors stand out. This effect works particularly well where text and background are similar and also has the benefit of generating smaller file sizes than the use of a more contrasting color.

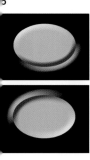

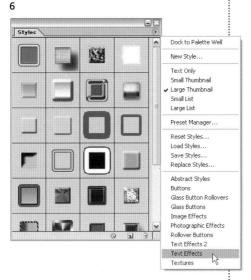

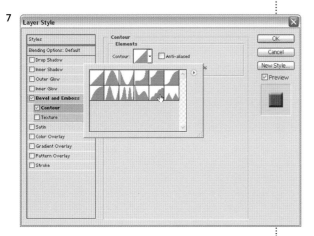

The same styles can also be used to create Web navigation buttons with a 3D appearance (5). By reversing the lighting you can also make buttons appear recessed or depressed. You will learn how to use this effect later with rollovers to simulate button-pressing when a mouse is rolled over the button.

Styles palette

The *Styles* palette gives you the chance to apply compound effects by clicking on a selected style or dragging and dropping it onto a selection. Click on the arrowhead to open the submenu and gain access to additional galleries of styles.

Like *Effects* in Elements (see page 126), adding a style to an image involves adding more than one effect. These are listed in the *Layers* palette. To remove a style you will need to remove each of the components individually by dragging them to the trash can.

The *Bevel and Emboss* dialog enables the type of bevel or emboss to be set, along with the extent of the effect required and lighting angles. Note the submenu *Contour* and *Texture* items in the *Styles* menu. To change the edge contour of the bevel, click on the submenu name and choose a contour from the pulldown menu. To apply this contour ensure that you have checked the box next to the submenu name.

1 *Inner Glow*

2 *Inner Shadow*

3 *Outer Glow*

4 *Layer Style Bevel and Emboss effects*

5 *Buttons Style Palette*

6 *Lighting change on bevelled navigation button*

7 *Contour and Texture submenu*

8 *Lighting and shadow submenu*

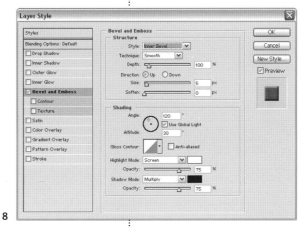

132 EXTRACT COMMAND

The *Extract* command is a sophisticated masking feature that enables accurate selections of subjects that are difficult to select with other tools. Similar to the *Magnetic Lasso*, the *Extract* command works by detecting the edge of the subject, but here the user can use a smart highlighter, which is a broad brush, to draw roughly around the subject.

1 Here's a particularly shaggy example of a subject that would be difficult to select using conventional tools. Select *Extract* (*Filter* > **Extract**) to open the dialog box.

2 Select the *Highlighter Pen* and draw around the edge of the subject. You can vary the width of the pen to ensure you cover all the subject edge, including any fine details such as the hair.

3 Use the *Fill* tool to fill the area bounded by the high-lighter. This will ensure that you have created a closed boundary around the subject.

4 Select *Preview* to preview the extraction. You can make fine corrections using the *Eraser* tool in the toolbar.

5 Save the image.

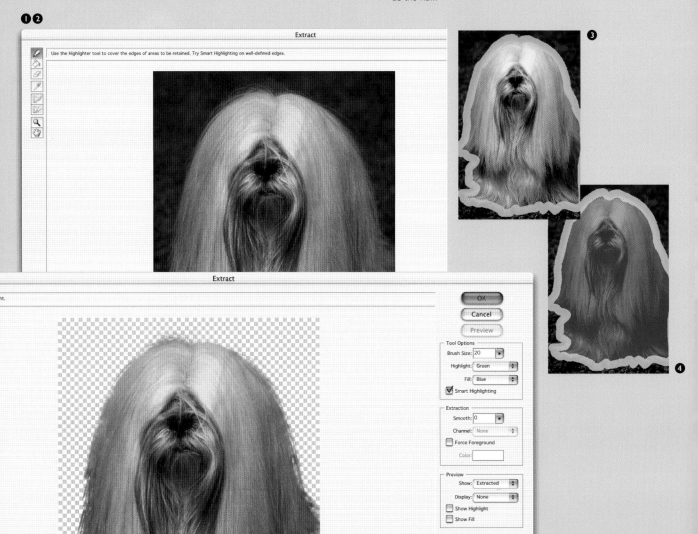

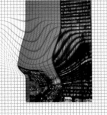

5

LIQUIFY

The *Liquify* command (within the *Filter* menu) is a freeform warping feature. A range of image distortions can be applied by dragging or stamping with one of tools provided.

You can control the size of the brush used to apply each effect, along with the pressure. There is also a *Reconstruct* tool to correct any mistakes or remove unwanted effects.

6

8

10

7

9

11

1	*Warp tool*	**7**	*Shift Pixels tool*
2	*Turbulence tool*	**8**	*Reflection tool*
3	*Twirl Clockwise tool*	**9**	*Reconstruct tool*
4	*Twirl Counter clockwise tool*	**10**	*Freeze tool*
5	*Pucker tool*	**11**	*Thaw tool*
6	*Bloat tool*		

134   PATTERN MAKER

The *Pattern Maker* plug-in debuted in Photoshop 7 and is ideal for creating patterns from a selection taken from an image. Unlike *Tile Maker*, which replicates a rectangular selection repeatedly over the screen, *Pattern Maker* uses a sophisticated analysis process to produce a pattern that is both seamless and avoids undue repetition.

You can use *Pattern Maker* to create realistic or abstract patterns. Realistic patterns could, for example, include a field of grass or a cloudscape generated from a small selection within an existing image. More original, abstract backgrounds can be produced from a different selection or by setting the *Pattern Maker* parameters to different values.

This makes *Pattern Maker* an obvious choice for generating unusual backgrounds for webpages. Because the new image is a non-repeated element, the file size of the pattern image will be larger than that of a traditional tile, but as the whole image contains the same color palette as the selection, that file size will still be smaller than that of a background graphic.

❶

❷

❸

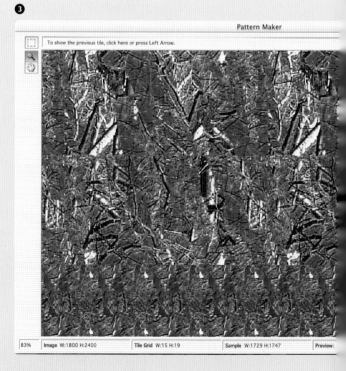

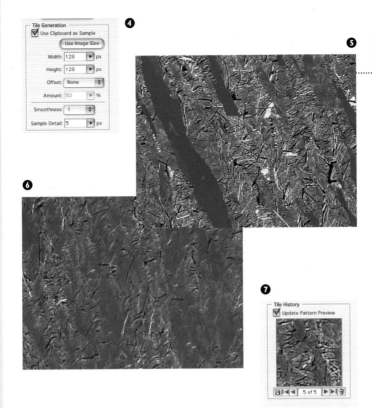

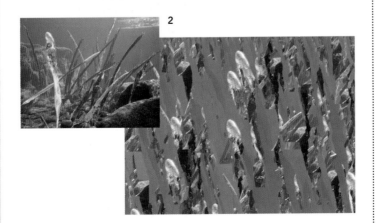

1 | **2** | **3** *The randomizing effect of this plug-in means that results can be unpredictable, so it is recommended that you create alternate patterns (using different settings) and compare the results before use. Here are some patterns and the original images from which they have been generated...*

Creating a pattern using Pattern Maker

❶ Select and open an image containing the element from which you intend to produce your pattern. Here we've used an image of a birch tree.

❷ Open the Pattern Maker. Select *Filter* > **Pattern Maker**. The selected image appears in the central pane.

❸ Draw a selection over the image (using the *Marquee* tool provided in the dialog box) to define the area you wish to use to generate the pattern. Press *Generate*. A pattern based on this selection and these settings is produced.

❹ To generate an alternate pattern select *Preview* > *Original* and then set new parameters in the *Tile Generation* box.

❺ Low *Sample Detail* (three pixels) and *Smoothness* (one) settings produce a more finely detailed pattern. The result is an abstract, splintered image.

❻ With higher settings (of nine pixels and three respectively), a softer result is produced. If used as a webpage background softer settings (with the smoothness set to three) will produce smaller overall file sizes. The result here emulates the look of fractured stone.

❼ You can continue to create new patterns by returning to the original image (as in step 4) and reconfiguring the parameters. Each time you do so the previous pattern is added to a 'library' that can be reviewed (and restored) using the *Tile History* window. Click on the buttons to scan through the saved patterns.

¹³⁶ IMAGE MONTAGE

Montage is another of those Photoshop techniques that, to explore fully, would require at least one full volume (probably more). The combining of elements from disparate sources is one of those tasks for which Photoshop is best suited. For Web use, image montages are often used for page backgrounds, image maps, and illustrations. There is nothing difficult about image montage and many of the pivotal techniques have already been explored. In fact, montage is one of those processes that requires a creative eye as much as it does technical prowess.

The Paris website

Imagine you are creating a personal website to illustrate Paris. The ultimate aim is to create a front page where visitors can click on scenes that link directly to a webpage telling them more about the location featured, and leading them on to further pictures of the city.

Begin by collecting images from all the scenes you would like to incorporate in this opening montage. Your choice will ultimately be dictated by the nature and aims of your website.

For now, go for a simple, plain background but, for visual interest, add a little texture.

TIP

Visual tricks

Clarity is the byword when conceiving website graphics. It must be obvious to a visitor what the options are and what your site is all about. So it is important to be able to construct a montage that doesn't compromise usability. There are two tricks we've use to great effect here. One is to reduce the opacity of the layers to help them blend together and with the background. The second is to add layer styles. Drop shadows lift objects from the background, while *Outer Glow*, which is applied to the text, separates the text by giving a gradient to white against the text. (You can also make extensive use of feathering to blend objects together seamlessly to create continuous backgrounds.)

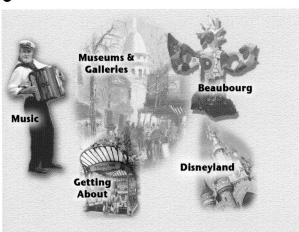

1 Create a new image. You might want to make this a convenient size for a webpage (say 600 by 800 pixels at 72 dpi) or make it larger and rescale it later. Use the *Texturizer* filter (*Filter > Texture > Texturizer*), set to *Canvas* to give the plain background a little more interest.

2 to **7** Now gather together the images that you'd like to use in your montage. To follow this example try to use the same ones that are used here, or similar ones. You won't be using the whole of the images, just elements from within each.

8 Begin with the picture of the jolly accordion player. Isolate him from the background by using the *Extract* command.

9 Paste him onto the background. It is unlikely that you'll get the size right first time —adjust the image size (or resolution) until you have the required result.

This is what your man will look like against the background.

10 Now add the image of the Disneyland castle. Place this in the bottom right-hand corner. For good composition, reverse the image first. Select *Image > Rotate Canvas > Flip Horizontal*.

11 This time don't cut out the castle, but give the image a soft edge. Select a feather radius (from the *Tool Options* bar) with the *Lasso* tool selected. Draw roughly around the outside of the castle edges to get the required soft edge.

12 Paste this onto the background.

13 Continue with the other image elements. To differentiate between elements, add a drop shadow to the accordion player and the fountain sculpture. Reduce the opacity of the layer containing the painting vignette so that it merges more into the background.

14 With all the pieces in place you can fine tune their relative positions by selecting the layer corresponding with the element and then repositioning that element. It is a good idea to decrease the opacity on each layer to help them blend together and with the background.

15 Now add the text that will enable visitors to your site to get around. Add this along with a layer style (*Outer Glow*) to increase the visual separation of the text and background.

Save the image when you are happy with the composition. Ensure that you save it in native Photoshop (PSD format) so that, should you wish to change it later, you have access to all the layers and effects applied.

138   More uses for montage

You can also use the same montage techniques to provide a composite seamless background to a webpage. In the following example we have compiled a montage that was used as a background graphic to several pages in a commercial website. Get together a few images on a similar theme and give it a try yourself.

T I P

Thumbnail montage

When you create a montage there are no rights and wrongs. And there is also a variety of styles that can deliver equally good results. As part of the creation of the "Sue Margaret" website the designers also produced an alternative based purely on thumbnails of the same images used in the montage.

This montage uses only layers with *Drop Shadow* and *Inner Glow* added to the text to improve the appearance.

❶❷❸❹ Start by collecting the images to be used. You many need to trim them or alter their size prior to building the montage. Laying them out roughly on screen is a useful way of seeing if any alteration is needed.

❺ Assemble the montage. Feather the edges of several selections but also make hard-edged selections so that some images are obviously above (in layer terms) others.

Save the image as a Photoshop format file. Then save a copy and flatten the layers (*Layers > Flatten Image*). Select Image > *Adjustments* > **Desaturate** to convert the image to black and white.

❻ Apply a filter to soften the image slightly and to help cover any unsightly joins. In this case we used Spatter.

❼ To convert the image to a background you need to color it. Use *Image > Adjustment > Hue/Saturation*. Click on the *Colorize* button and adjust *Hue*.

❽ Reduce the contrast and increase the brightness using the *Brightness/Contrast* command.

❾ Here's what the example page looked like on the real website. The text was stored as part of the image on this introductory page in order that the special font—Lydian ITC, the client's preferred choice—and color could be easily included.

❿ *Photoshop can open native Illustrator files (files created in Illustrator's own format). If you open one you'll see the Rasterize Generic EPS Format dialog box open. Enter the required dimensions and resolution and press OK (or use the default settings, shown in the dialog box).*

⓫ *Here's how the Illustrator sample image Chinese Opera appears after being rasterized in Photoshop.*

USING VECTOR GRAPHICS WITHIN PHOTOSHOP

Vector graphics, created in Adobe Illustrator (or perhaps Macromedia Freehand), can be imported into Photoshop.

For applications other than Illustrator and, in particular, those that do not offer a format directly compatible with Photoshop, you should save your artwork in EPS (encapsulated PostScript) format. This is because most EPS files can be opened successfully in Photoshop.

Exporting from Illustrator

You can export an image from Illustrator in rasterized form, ready to use in Photoshop. It's better, though, to rasterize an Illustrator graphic in Photoshop, since you can retain the transparent areas in an image (such as the border of the Chinese Opera image shown here). Files exported from Illustrator have transparent areas rendered to white.

You may be wondering why you would want to use vector graphics within Photoshop. Despite all its power and scope, which does include some vector tools, Photoshop lacks a few illustrative tools that professional illustrators demand. For example, features such as writing text along a path are easy to do in Illustrator but impossible in Photoshop.

If you don't have Illustrator then don't worry—virtually all the effects shown in this book presume you'll be working only with Photoshop.

140   IMAGE SECURITY

It's inevitable that the Internet, the means by which we share information on an unparalleled scale, also provides an easy way for the unscrupulous to steal work. When it comes to website design and design features you need to approach the subject of theft of your intellectual property with a degree of resignation. If your website boasts eye-catching, effective graphics, then you should treat plagiarism as a compliment. And, to be honest, if someone uses your ideas and implements them in a website, unless it relates to a subject similar to yours, there will be little harm done. If it does relate to a similar subject, then there's a strong chance that visitors will have seen your offering first.

The theft of images via the Web is much more serious, however. Increasingly the Web is the delivery medium for images, and the nature of digital media means that an image you send in good faith can be misused by whoever receives it. Although nothing is foolproof, there are ways and means to reduce the risk. Here are a few points to keep in mind if you send images by email or are considering posting valuable images on your site.

- Add a visible copyright notice to the print. It indicates that you are alert to image theft (though can be removed with careful cloning).
- Make only low-resolution images available on a website. Visitors who wish to get hold of a high-resolution version can then have this emailed to them—subject to payment or copyright agreement, of course.
- Embed a digital watermark in the image. Photoshop offers the *Digimarc* watermarking facility (see box for details). This improves security, but the process is not infallible.
- Create a limited access website. Only authorized people can visit, and you determine the terms by which they are able to. This restricts access so that only those with a genuine interest enter but also limits the number of visitors. Some will no doubt be put off by your security measures!
- Slicing images also offers a partial deterrent because each slice has to be downloaded separately and then reassembled.

❶

❷

Digimarc digital watermarking

The *Digimarc* filter (at the base of the *Filters* menu) embeds a digital watermark into your image, which is encoded into its structure. Although the watermark is notionally invisible, there is a minor amount of image degradation. The Filter control lets you choose between a less visible (and less durable) watermark, and a more visible but more durable offering. Less durable watermarks are slightly less able to survive image manipulations.

When an image with a Digimarc watermark is opened (as it might be on a recipient's computer) the watermark is detected and the information (normally as to the originator of the image) is displayed.

To use *Digimarc* you must register with the Digimarc Corporation. This is partly a means of funding the watermarking business, but it also helps to keep tabs on your images if someone unexpectedly finds an image with your watermark.

Embedding a watermark

Creating first-line protection with an embedded copyright notice is easy: simply add a type layer with a copyright notice. However, this is generally too brusque a method, so using a blending mode can be more effective.

❶ Type a copyright notice across your image. Make it large enough to be significant but not so large as to compromise the image. In particular, avoid overwriting important parts of the image.

❷❸ Select Layer Styles (*Layers > Layer Styles > Blending Options*) and a *Blend* mode (good ones are *Soft Light* and *Color Dodge*). The effects vary depending on the underlying image. In the first of these examples *Soft Light* has been used; in the second *Color Dodge* was employed, with opacity reduced to 50 percent.

❸

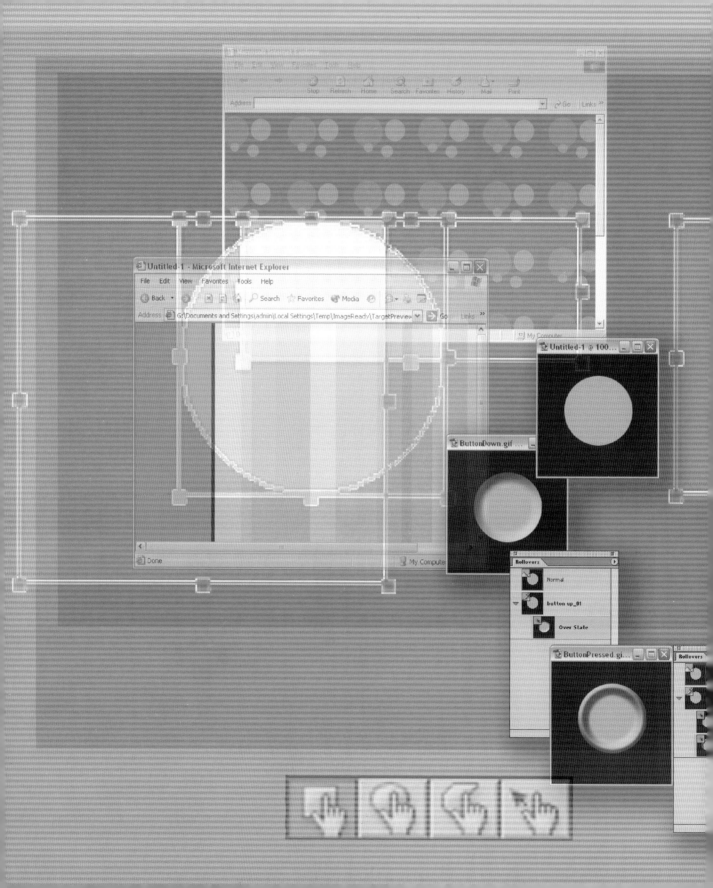

CHAPTER 6

Creating Web Elements

A great deal of good Web design goes largely unnoticed. This is partly testament to the good design: users feel so comfortable in the environment created for them that they don't give it a second thought. Think about the last five websites that you visited. Can you remember the screen backgrounds that were used? What navigational aids and button types were used? In this section we'll look at the components of a website. Some are purely graphical—background images and artwork, for example. Others, like image slices and image maps, are concerned with the engineering and construction of the website.

144 WEB BACKGROUNDS: STARTING FROM THE BACK

We all visit websites for the most part with the aim of finding information. The "paper" on which the information is presented is of no interest. So should that mean the background of a webpage should be plain or simply ignored by the webpage designer? Many commentators think that it should. However, far more people, including those that create and use websites, think differently and the consensus is that backgrounds are an important feature that contributes to a website's character and style.

The background on backgrounds

What, precisely is a Web background? Visually, it is the background image of a webpage that all images, graphics, and text are placed on. In terms of website mechanics this is an HTML feature that provides us with the facility to place an image beneath the other content of the page.

Any image file can form the basis of a background. You've seen how a montage graphic was produced with the sole purpose of providing a webpage background (although because it had active elements and was not generic, it was not a background in the strictest interpretation of the term). Web backgrounds can be saved as GIF, JPEG, or even PNG files and behave in exactly the same way as other images do.

1|2 *For a small file size, the original image needs to be optimized. In this case, the full-color image has been reduced to just the seven colors indicated on the color table in the* Save for Web *dialog.*

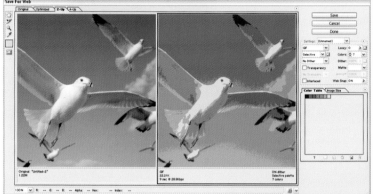

3 *The text 'Photographing Sea Birds' needs to be added. To create the translucent 'watermark' effect, the type layer has been blended with the background image layer using the* Soft Light *blend mode, altering the transparency until the desired degree of transparency is achieved.*

TIP

Don't let your background dominate!

It is important to remember that a background is just that—a background. It is there to help display the contents of your webpage. Bright colors and bold designs will compete for attention with your content, and any website visitors will feel such competition acutely. Keep this in mind at all times!

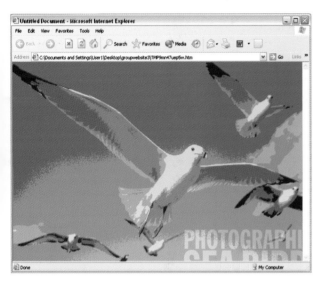

Background images differ from other images purely in the way—by virtue of the HTML that underpins them—the browser displays them. In particular, a browser will tile an image horizontally and vertically in order to fill the space available. So you can make background images large (larger even than a browser window might be expected to be), but you can also create small, iconic images that can be tiled across the screen no matter how the browser window is scaled.

7
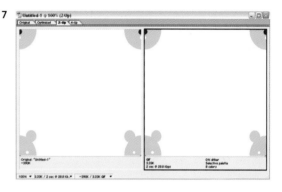

4 *You can now use the* Preview in Browser *button to check how the image will look in the browser. In this case the browser window is slightly larger than the 800 x 600 pixel background image, and so the repeated, tiled patern is visible.*

6 *Here's how to tile a simple graphic (made from a group of ellipses) so that it occupies the entire browser window, including the edges and the corner. Start by applying the* Offset *filter, set to 50% Horizontal and 50% Vertical.*

5 *Assuming you are happy with the browser results, your background is ready to use. It's worth looking at the results using different browser window sizes to ensure nothing crucial gets lost!*

7 *The offset has moved the graphic so that a proportion of it appears in the corner of each tile. Ensure the image is optimized in such a way that it is as compact as possible.*

8
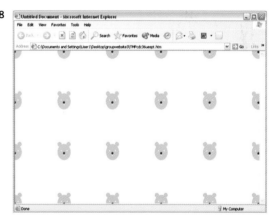

8 *When previewed in the selected browser, you can see that the pattern fills the browser window from the top left-hand corner.*

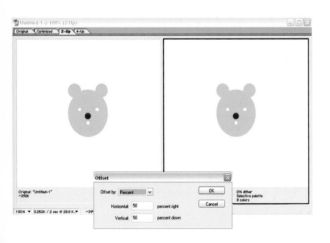

146 Creating your first background

To best understand how a graphic is interpreted as
a background, you should first try creating a simple
tiled background.

❶ In Photoshop (or
ImageReady) choose *File >
New* to open the *New
Document* dialog box. Enter
a size (around 1½ inches
square is ideal) at the screen
resolution of 72dpi.

❷ Use the *Painting* or *Fill*
tools to add a simple design
to the image. This needn't be
anything too elaborate. Here
we've used just three colors,
the *Fill* tool, and the
Rectangular Marquee.

A good design tip is to keep the
design away from the edges of
the image and to have the
same solid color around all the
edges. This can be by means
of a frame or by virtue of
keeping the background color.
This makes the tiling more
effective and seamless.

Once you are happy with your
graphic, save it and, if you are
using Photoshop, *Jump To*
ImageReady.

❸ Use the *Optimize* options to
select the file compressions. (For
this example it is not crucial to
optimize precisely, although it is
good practice to do so).

❹ Select *File > Output
Settings > Background*.
Choose *Background* for the
View Document As option in
the *Output Settings* dialog box.
The appropriate HTML code will
now be created and appended
to the image, specifying this as
a background image.

Click on the *Preview in Browser*
button in the toolbar to display
your background. Note that you
also have the corresponding
HTML code displayed.

Using the Tile Maker to prepare an image for use in a background

ImageReady features a filter for creating tiles
from existing graphics or images. You'll find
Tile Maker in the Filters > *Other* submenu.
Here's how it works.

❶ Open a portion of the image
"Dune", which you'll find in
Photoshop's Samples folder.

❷ Use the *Rectangular
Marquee* to make a selection
from the image for use as the
background tile. This can be as
small or large as you wish.

Choose *Filter > Other >
Tile Maker*.

❸ Set *Filter Options* in the
dialog box.

Enter a blend amount for the
tile edges. This will determine
the degree to which edges are
blended to make the tile more
seamless. Normally an amount

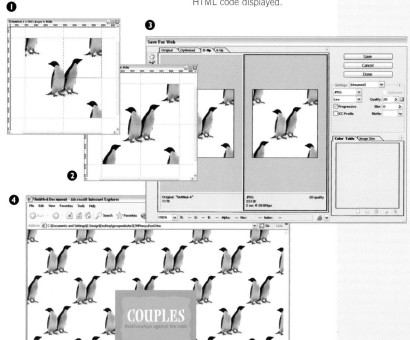

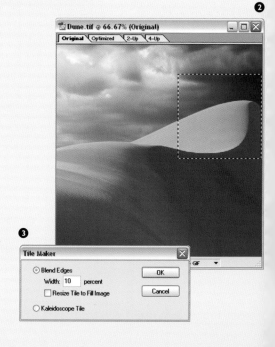

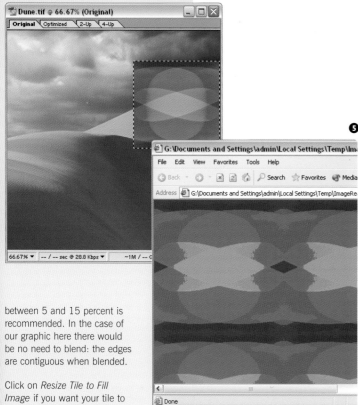

❹

❺

between 5 and 15 percent is recommended. In the case of our graphic here there would be no need to blend: the edges are contiguous when blended.

Click on *Resize Tile to Fill Image* if you want your tile to be expanded to the size of the original image.

❹ Select *Kaleidoscope* Tile if you want adjacent tiles to be flipped horizontally and/or vertically to create a more abstract pattern. This will render the graphic sand dune form into a graphic pattern.

Click *OK* to create your tile.

Choose *Image > Crop* to crop the image to the selection (unless you are using the entire image area as a selection).

Select *File > Output Settings > Background*. Choose *Background* for the *View As* option in the *Output Settings* dialog box. The appropriate HTML code will now be created and appended to the image, as it was in the previous example.

❺ Preview the image in a browser.

❷ Crop the image. This is your tile. You can now optimize and use the techniques above to place it as your background. Note the HTML code generated.

Sidebar backgrounds

The use of a sidebar as a means of gathering together navigational tools has been a design feature of many websites since their earliest days. And, because such a layout is, in fact, very useful this has avoided the pitfall of many designs—becoming clichéd. It also has the added benefit of requiring only a small, compact graphic that can be tiled across the sidebar.

To make a sidebar background:

Begin by creating a new image file in ImageReady to the width of the webpage (or greater). Use a nominal width of 1,200 pixels. It isn't as important to get the height correct, since you'll be using tiling to take care of the vertical dimensions.

❶ Color in the main background and add a sidebar using the Rectangular Marquee, and infilling with a second color of your choice.

Make a horizontal selection using the Marquee again. This needs to be to the full width of the window and around 25 pixels deep.

❶

❷

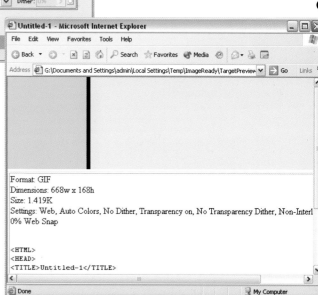

148 Full-sized backgrounds

You can make your tile any size. Theoretically a
single pixel could be tiled, but it is normal to choose
something larger to prevent diverting too much
computing power to the tiling process.

At the other end of the scale, tiles can be so
large that effectively only one, or even part of one,
forms the background. It would be an easy project
to create such a tile (and could produce a rather
elegant effect) were it not for the fact that there is
no standard browser window size. Many browsers
have a default size to which they first open
following the software installation, but the needs
of the user and of specific webpages will mean
that this size is quickly changed. Some assumptions
have to be made, therefore. In particular, assume
an optimum browser window size of around 1,024
x 768 pixels. This is a fair assumption given the
size and resolution of contemporary monitors.
Many people will not be able to view a window of
this size and there will be even fewer whose
browser windows are larger.

You do need to be particularly mindful of those
with smaller monitors when designing a large
graphic. Large image tiles are pasted from the top
left-hand corner of the browser window (rather than
centrally) so in a window smaller than the image,
the right-hand and bottom edges will be trimmed.
If you are aiming to create a full background image
that will fill any browser without tiling, use a basic
image size of around 1,200 x 800 pixels. This will
fill even the largest standard browser window.

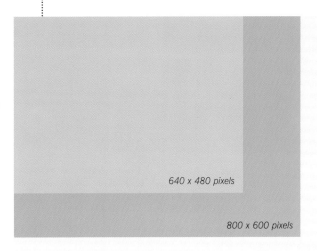

640 x 480 pixels

800 x 600 pixels

1024 x 768 pixels

1

1 *Viewers with smaller browser
windows will see proportionately
less of the background graphic.
It is important therefore that
the missing areas do not
contain anything too important.
At the risk of compromising
creativity, it can be a wise
move to include (or duplicate)
navigation controls toward the
top or left of the screen.*

2 *JavaScript.com.*

TIP

Forcing window sizes

Where it is important to your site that the browser
window size matches the size of the background
image, you can use HTML and JavaScript to control
the browser window. Pay a visit to websites that
specialize in JavaScript to see how this is achieved.
Some of these feature JavaScript routines that can
be copied into the HTML code of your site. Set your
search engine to work with the keyword "JavaScript"
and see what sites come up. **JavaScript.com** is one
of the more comprehensive.

2

Integral tiling

In addition to using tiling to repeat a background image to form a continuous pattern, you can use this feature to create a background that is an integral part of your layout.

① Create a new document sized 1000 x 100 pixels. Divide it in half vertically. Using the *Marquee* tool, define an area at the top of 300 x 50 pixels. Fill this with color and to use the *Sponge* filter to add texture.

② Duplicate the area and apply *Transform > Flip Horizontal*. Now butt these two areas together. Use the *Pencil* tool to draw a horizontal line beneath. Finally, fill the bottom half with color. When repeated, no joins will be visible.

③ Use *Save for Web* if you are in Photoshop, or *Save Optimized* if you are in ImageReady. Select GIF and reduce the colours to a minimum. In this example, 16 was adequate, resulting in a file size of just under 10kb.

④ Using your Web design application, insert the GIF as a background image.

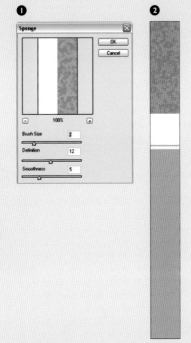
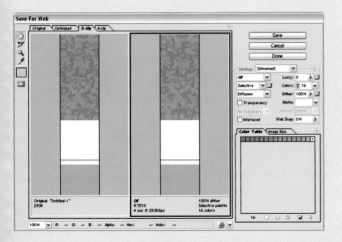

The use of large graphics as backgrounds has been—and remains—controversial. Many Web designers avoid their use on the perfectly valid basis that an image large enough to fill a space of 1,200 x 800 pixels will still take some time to download. We can compress the image (and use other "dodges" such as blurring the image slightly) to reduce the file size and make the download more expedient, but whether this is sufficient to prevent site visitors from surfing onward to another site is debateable. There is no doubt however that a large graphic—whether used as the subject of the webpage or as the background—can be imposing and make the webpage equally so.

It is perhaps important to ask yourself whether your website will truly benefit from a large single graphic. If the answer is yes, go ahead and use one. If not, a tiled alternative should suffice. Don't forget either that backgrounds don't have to include an image; some pages—particularly text-heavy ones—benefit from a neutral backing.

Background Cheats

If you are concentrating on creating the content of your website you might want to forego the additional complication of creating backgrounds. The Web is awash with sites offering free backgrounds for your site—both as tiles and as full screens. The drawback of using a readymade background (or, indeed, any readymade element) is that it can detract from the uniqueness of your site. Chances are the best backgrounds will have also been adopted by others.

Don't forget that a visit to one of these sites is an excellent way of looking at how tiled backgrounds can be made to look like a single image, and successful background images can be compressed and still be meaningful.

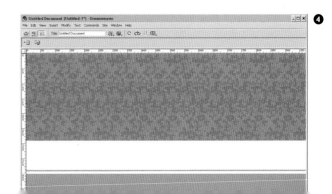

150 BUTTONS

Buttons are the simplest of all navigational tools. Click on a button and you are taken (by virtue of the link attached to it) to a new page or location. Multiple Web elements are involved, but the first —and most visible—is the button itself.

To create your own working buttons you need an understanding of some graphical tools. This will help you to create a visually attractive range. You also need to discover how the graphic or image on which the buttons have been placed can be broken into "sensitized" areas, so that a link to the location it respresents can be activated. Finally, you need to provide some feedback for the user. When a button is pressed, as with the click of a keyboard key, you need to indicate to the user that the button has been successfully pressed and that the process it activates is underway.

Creating a basic button

In Web terms a button is no more than a defined area of the screen that the user clicks on to initiate an action. A piece of text, element of an image, or patch of color can all be defined as, and act as, buttons. But when designing a website for mass appeal it makes sense to create buttons that are instantly recognizable as such. Use the steps below to create a simple raised button, then modify it to create a pressed button effect. You can use this same pair of images later with rollovers to give the impression that a button has been pressed when the mouse is passed over it.

❶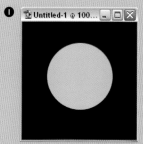

❷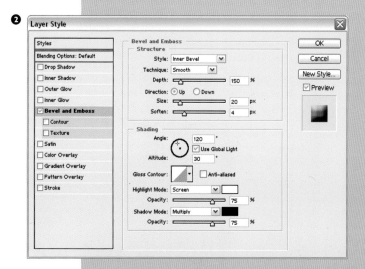

① Create a new document and, in a new layer, draw a simple shape such as a circle, square, or ellipse with the *Marquee* tool. If you want to create a square or circle hold down the shift key as you drag with the *Rectangular* or *Elliptical Marquee* respectively.

Fill the selection with a mid-toned color.

② Select *Layer > Layer Styles > Bevel and Emboss* to open the *Bevel and Emboss* dialog box. Use these layer styles to give the impression of a 3D button (see *right*).

③ Adjust the *Size* and the *Soften* parameters to give your button edge a rounded look. The lighting effect gives the button a raised appearance.

Save this image for future use as a JPEG or (more appropriate in this case) a GIF file. Give it a recognizable name such as "Button Up".

④ Open the *Bevel and Emboss* dialog box again. Find the *Direction* options and click on the *Down* radio button. The lighting has changed to give the impression that the button is concave.

Save this button as "Button Down".

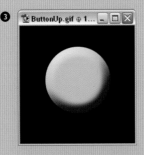

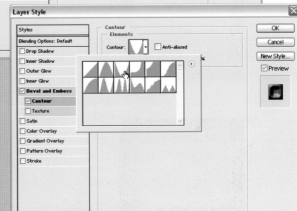

More complex button designs

The *Bevel and Emboss* dialog box has a further feature that can give give your creation an even more authentic button effect.

Create a raised button as you did for the basic button (or simply open your saved copy of "Button Up").

① Open the *Layer Styles* dialog box again and select *Bevel and Emboss* and click on the *Down* radio button. Click on the small check box under *Bevel and Emboss*, which is marked *Contour*, then doubleclick on the word *Contour* to the right of the box. The *Contour* panel will display in the dialog box.

② Click on the arrowhead to open the *Contours* palette. This gives you the choice of using different edge profiles (contours) for your buttons.

③ Choose an alternate contour —one that gives a very effective "pressed button" look is called *Inverted Cone*.

Save the new button with the name "Button Pressed".

152 **Round-cornered buttons**

Photoshop and ImageReady are great for producing elliptical and rectangular buttons but, until the launch of version 6 and onward (and Photoshop Elements), were poor at creating round-cornered buttons. Various contrived ways were expounded for creating them but none of these justified the time and effort involved, at least for the average user.

Now, though, round-cornered buttons are as easy to create as any other type.

Create a new image and add a new layer, as before.

❶ Select the *Rounded Rectangle* tool. This is one of the *Vector Shape* tools. To select it click on the *Vector* tool button and select the rounded rectangle from the *Tool Options* bar or select from the pullout menu on the toolbar.

Select your fill color (When you draw an object with a vector tool the shape is automatically filled with the current foreground color.)

Select a radius for the corners using the setting on the *Tool Options* bar. This will depend on the size of your button; draw some test boxes with different radiuses to see how this works.

❷ Draw your box (it will automatically fill with color).

❸❹ Apply layer styles as before.

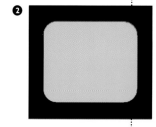

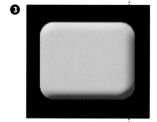

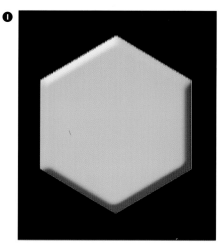

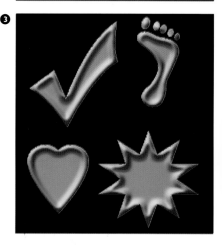

Creating buttons with vector tools

In the same way that you used the rounded rectangle to create a button, you can use any of the vector tools to create button shapes.

❶ Here the *Polygonal* tool was used to create a hexagonal button.

❷❸ The *Shape* tool offers a range of preformed shapes that can form the basis of your buttons. Stars, tick marks, hearts, and as here, footprints, can all be used along with any unique shapes you care to create...

Button shortcuts

The *Styles* palette offers a range of button effects that can be easily applied to a shape or selection. As we saw earlier, *Styles* is nothing more than a sequenced amalgam of several layer styles or effects but this makes them no less valuable. Use the pullout menu on the *Styles* palette to review the options in the *Buttons, Glass Buttons,* and *Glass Button Rollover* menus.

1 Buttons.

2 Glass Buttons. (Glass Button Rollovers *offers a similar set.)*

1

2

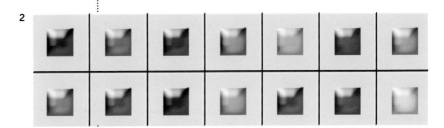

154 IMAGE SLICES

We've talked about making a button "work" by making it active. The feature used for this is image slicing. Slices offer the means by which a Photoshop image can be turned into a useful webpage graphic. When an image is sliced into smaller components it becomes possible to redefine sections of the image and apply particular Web elements, such as rollovers. Though the physical (if that is an appropriate term in a virtual world!) integrity of an image remains even when it is sliced, a sliced image is regarded in HTML terms as a set of images and each part is stored as a separate graphics file. Behind the scenes, when you slice an image, a table is created in HTML that describes how the sliced image should be reassembled. Usefully, when an image is sliced, individual slices can be saved using different optimization regimes. You can even save some elements in JPEG and others in GIF format.

You can work with slices in either Photoshop or ImageReady, because there are similar creative tools provided in each. However, while images in Photoshop need not include a slice, every ImageReady image will feature at least one slice. Where no slice has been drawn, the entire image will comprise a single slice.

Note that slices are, without exception, square or rectangular. However, by adding transparency to them, they can also be made to appear more irregularly shaped.

❶ Select *Toggle Slices Visibility* on the ImageReady menu and at least one slice will be displayed for every image (in Photoshop you need to select *View > Show > Slices*).

❷❸ We will see later that creating slices is easy. By defining an area that we wish to make into a slice, Photoshop (or ImageReady) will automatically create slices around that slice so that the entire image is divided into a number of rectangular slices. These slices will be modified if we subsequently draw another slice, as we can see in these two illustrations.

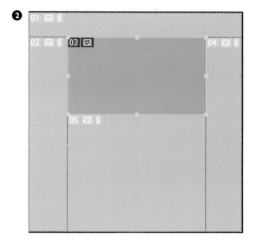

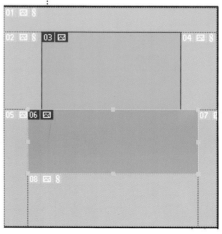

Slices versus image maps

To the visitor of a website a sliced image and an image map appear to operate in much the same way, particularly when links are similarly attached. A sliced image, as we have seen, is a single image that has been cut into elements, which can be addressed separately. Links can be attached to elements and rollovers applied to each.

An image map begins as, and remains, a single image file in which certain areas have been defined as link areas. HTML code defines these regions and is stored with the image. Unlike slices, you can create image maps of any shape and also define link areas in any shape.

❶

❶ An original image. The text has been typed in the type layer and stroked (*Layer > Layer Style > Stroke*) to give it a crisp and clear outline.

❷

❷ This is the sliced image version with the slices made visible. Each slice has a separate link attached to it and is saved as a separate graphics file. Note how auto-slices (see *right*) have been created outside the user-slices corresponding to the navigation areas.

❸

❸ An image map. The area of, and around, each piece of text is the active area. When this is clicked on, it takes the visitor to the link location. Although indicated by a marquee in this illustration, the user would see an image identical to the original.

Types of slice

There are several slice types. Some are user-created, while others are produced automatically.

User-Slice This type of slice is generated when you use a slicing tool. You can select a user-slice in which resizing/reshaping handles (akin to those that appear on a crop selection) appear.

Auto-Slice When you create a user-slice in an image, an auto-slice is created automatically. The auto-slice is required for reconciling the HTML table that stores the slice information. Auto-slices account for those areas of an image that are not accounted for by user- or other slices. They are regenerated each time a user- (or layer-based) slice is added to an image or the size of an existing slice is changed.

Layer-based Slice Created from layers, layer-based slices will auto-adjust their size to encompass the entire pixel data of a layer. Make any changes to the layer, and the slice will adjust its dimensions to accommodate them.

Subslice Another automatically created slice, this is generated when you allow two slices to overlap. You cannot select or edit a subslice, even though it features the standard slice symbol and is numbered. Subslices will be regenerated in response to any changes to other slices.

No Image Slice A slice defined as a No Image slice has no graphic file associated with it. No Image slices occur when slicing an image creates areas that are nominally empty. Of course, they are not actually empty, but contain solid (probably background) color. A "spacer" GIF file is added to the HTML table. The benefit of using a No Image Slice is that it can speed up download times.

156 Slicing in Photoshop and ImageReady

Both Photoshop and ImageReady provide tools
for the creation of image slices. The *Slice* and
Slice Select tools (which share a menu position)
are featured in the toolbox of both programs.
ImageReady also features a *Slice Visibility* icon
(below the foreground/background color swatches).

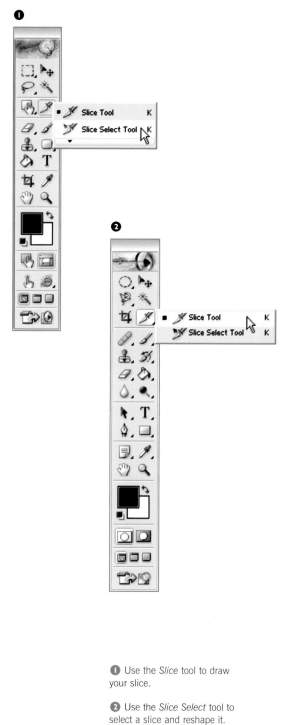

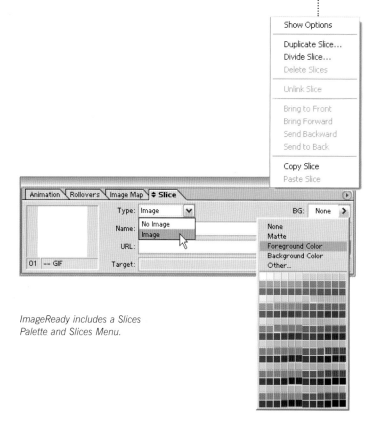

*ImageReady includes a Slices
Palette and Slices Menu.*

❶ Use the *Slice* tool to draw
your slice.

❷ Use the *Slice Select* tool to
select a slice and reshape it.

Creating and selecting slices

Slices are easily created. If you prefer to work freehand, you can choose the *Slice* tool and drag the slice boundary in the same way that you use the *Rectangular Marquee*. In ImageReady you can use the *Rectangular Marquee* to make a selection the same size as the intended slice then select *Slices > Create Slice from Selection*.

When creating multiple slices that are adjacent to one another you'll find that new slice boundaries will snap to those of existing slices. This makes for a potentially neat arrangement of the slices and prevents the creation of anomalous auto-slices in the gaps between user-slices. Other auto-slices will be automatically generated.

❸ Here's an example of how to add slices to a menu of buttons.

❹ Select the *Slice* tool. When selected you will see a single auto-slice applied to the whole image (and indicated by the gray corner icon and number).

❺ Drag the *Slice* tool over the first button. A user-slice (numbered 3) is created. Note how the original auto-slice has been divided into smaller, complete rectangles, each of which is numbered separately.

❻ Starting from the bottom left-hand corner of your first user-slice, drag the *Slice* tool to create a second user-slice for the next button. You'll see how the new slice snaps to the edges of the first user-slice and the bounding auto-slices.

❼ Continue to add four user-slices corresponding to the four buttons.

To select a different slice:

❽ Select the *Slice Select* tool. This shares a toolbar location with the slice tool. Click on the tool to see the options and select the *Slice Select* tool.

Click on the slice to select it. (If you need to select multiple slices, hold down the *Shift* key and click on all the slices you want to select.)

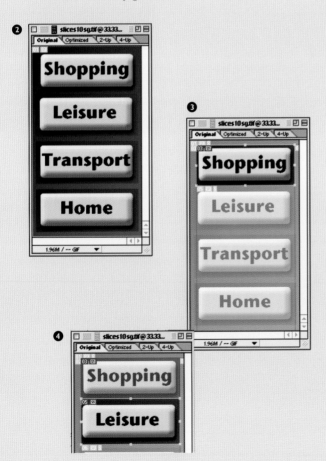

158 Slice manipulations

Here are some more things you can do with the slices that you've created.

Resizing a slice

Use the *Slice Select* tool and drag the corner and side handles. Remember that slices cannot overlap and they cannot be dragged into a shape that is not rectangular.

Create a layer-based slice

This is possible only in ImageReady. Select the layer in which you want to create a layer-based slice and choose *Layers* > **Create New Layer-Based Slice**. Remember that layer-based slices are created based on the contents of the layer, and comprise the smallest rectangle into which those contents will fit. Their size cannot be manually adjusted but they will be redrawn when the layer contents are modified.

Linking Slices

Two or more slices can be linked together by using the ImageReady command, *Slices* > **Link Slices**. Linking slices is a useful feature when it comes to optimizing. You can link together all the images and all the graphics and then optimize just once for each set.

Changing the status of a slice

You can change the status of a slice from its current setting to user-slice using the command *Promote to User-Slice*. This tool might be used if you wish to use (and perhaps manipulate) an auto-slice and change it to a user-slice.

Copying a slice

To apply the same slice structure to several images you can use the *Copy Slices* and *Paste Slices*. These features are all to be found in the ImageReady *Slices* menu.

Optimizing slices

One of the benefits of image slicing is the opportunity to save individual elements with different optimizations. You might, for example, optimize a photograph as a JPEG while the remainder of the image—a graphic—might be saved as a GIF. To optimize a slice, use the *Slice Select* tool to select a slice and then set the optimize parameters in the *Optimize* palette.

Strictly speaking, each slice in an image should have its own optimize settings, though each of these does not need to be unique. Typically professional Web designers have two default optimization settings, one for all the JPEG images and one for the GIF graphics. If you choose to do this, remember that you can save considerable time by linking all similar slices together first and then apply the optimizing settings to each linked set.

And don't forget that to view slices you need only click on the *Slice Visibility* icon in ImageReady or, in Photoshop, select *Show* > *Extras* > **Slices**.

TIP

Using Guides

It is important, to make your webpage download as fast as possible, to cut your image so that as few auto slices as possible are created. Using *Guides* is an excellent way of ensuring that your slices are set to the same alignment. You can create a guide by selecting *View* > **New Guide** and then specifying whether you wish a horizontal or vertical guide. Then drag the guide to the required position. Once you have set up a grid of guides at the appropriate positions you can create slices automatically. Select *Slices* > **Create Slice** from Guides. And if you need to combine these slices to make larger ones use *Slices* > **Combine slices**.

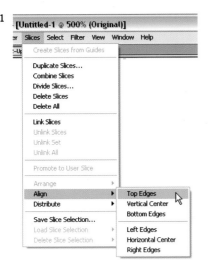

2

1 Align Slices *submenu.*

2 *These options are shown as icons in the ImageReady* Tool Options *bar when the* Select Slices *tool is selected and more than one slice is selected.*

3 *Adding a link to a slice.*

3

Arranging slices

Once you've got an image that is made up of multiple slices you may need to align and arrange them so that they are accurately positioned on the page. In ImageReady, with the slices you want to arrange selected, you can align or distribute all the edges, tops, or centers as required by selecting *Slices* > **Align** or *Slices* > **Distribute**. The options (which are the same for both align and distribute) are shown in a submenu.

Adding a link to a slice

Apart from differential optimizing, the principle reason for slicing an image is to create live buttons that, when pressed, open a connected webpage or website. This is achieved by assigning a URL, corresponding to that website or page, to the slice. Here's how to give your buttons a live link.

Select the slice you want to link from.

In the *Slice Options* dialog box (in Photoshop) or *Slice Palette* (in ImageReady) enter the URL of the link. You can use a relative or absolute URL (see below). The *Slice Options* dialog box can be easily opened by doubleclicking (with the *Slice Select* tool) on the slice. Click *OK*.

Absolute and relative URLs

An absolute URL is the exact location in the World Wide Web and will begin with a protocol, (usually) http://, a server name (www) and then a pathname and filename. For example an absolute URL of a particular image might be *http://www.myWebsite. com/images/2001/vacation/123456.jpg*.

Relative URLs do not feature either a protocol or a server name. These are used if the file is on the same computer or server as the original page that includes the link.

160   Web photo gallery

Hidden in Photoshop's (and Elements') *Automate* submenu (*File* > **Automate**) is the Web Photo Gallery. You can use this automated process to generate a Web photo gallery using your own images. The rigorously defined format means that you won't get a very original format, but it is certainly a quick and effective method to use. Here's how to create one.

Because it is an automated process, there is very little need for manual intervention. It is, however, important that you prepare your photographs correctly. You will need to ensure that the images are correctly captioned (filenames are used for captions) and that you have performed any appropriate edits on the images first.

In particular, you need to ensure that landscape and portrait shots are correctly oriented. Collect the images together in a single folder. (You can have multiple folders, but they need to be within one overall folder.)

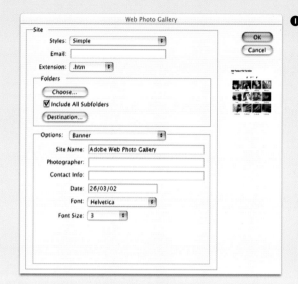

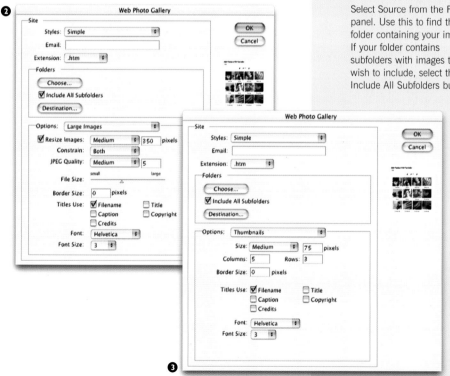

❶ Choose *File* > *Automate* > **Web Photo Gallery**.

Select Source from the Files panel. Use this to find the folder containing your images. If your folder contains subfolders with images that you wish to include, select the Include All Subfolders button.

Note that all files, whether from the folder or subfolders, will be listed alphabetically and no distinction is made in respect of their original location.

Select a destination. This can be an existing or new folder in which you wish to store the optimized images and the corresponding HTML.

Choose a style for the gallery. The thumbnail to the right of the dialog box previews the options available.

In *Options* you can have a banner (a site name, company name, or whatever you choose) that will appear on every page. Enter your chosen name for this gallery in the *Site Name* window. Give your, or the photographer's, name in the *Photographer* box. If you want the gallery dated, then add the date in the *Date* field (the current date appears by default). Select a font and font size for the text used. Note that you can leave any, or all, of these fields blank.

❷ Select *Large Images* from the *Options* popup menu. You can set a border size, resize images, and also set a JPEG compression setting here. It is usually best to retain the defaults for your first attempt then, after analyzing the results, make any changes you consider appropriate.

❸ Select *Thumbnails* from the same *Options* popup menu. You can configure the layout of the homepage here. Note that if you select *Titles Use Caption*,

there must be file information recorded along with the image.

You can set up colors for your Web gallery using the *Custom Colors* option from the popup menu. You can select any colors (not necessarily just Web-safe colors) by clicking on the color swatch.

Click *OK* to begin creating the gallery. When complete, your favored browser will launch and the Web gallery will appear.

You'll find the following in the folder specified as the *Destination*:

• An HTML document entitled *index.htm*, which is your homepage. You can open this in any browser.
• A subfolder containing HTML corresponding to each image (pages).
• The images themselves in optimized form (images).
• Image thumbnails for display on the homepage (thumbnails).
• An HTML document defining the image frames comprising the website.
• A text document, *UserSelections.txt*, with configuration parameters.

4 *Here are some examples of Web galleries taken from PictureCDs. Images were copied to the hard disk first in order that correct orientation could be established.*

5 *This gallery, created using the* Horizontal Frame *format, lets users click on an image in the lower gallery to see it, and its caption is displayed above.*

6 *In the alternative* Table *format the homepage displays thumbnails of all included images. Click on any of these to see the full-screen version.*

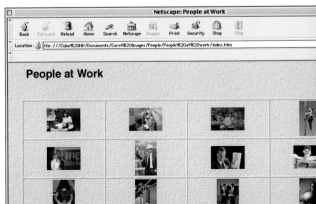

¹⁶² ROLLOVERS

Rollovers are one of the most common Web design features. A rollover is simply an element on a webpage that changes in some way when the mouse pointer passes over it. The change may be something as simple as a switch from standard to bold text, or more profound: a name changing to an image, for example. Others may open submenus of topics as you pass by, or feature buttons that seem to be pressed merely by the motion of your mouse. You can create the graphics for a rollover in Photoshop or ImageReady, but you'll need ImageReady's tools to engineer the rollover itself.

The engineering of a rollover involves the swapping of image files depending on the position and state of the mouse and a mouse event. ImageReady supports six such mouse events (see box). Rollover events are controlled by a JavaScript within the HTML of the webpage —this code is generated within ImageReady.

The purpose of a rollover is principally one of communication. The placing of a rollover on a webpage indicates to the user that the word or image they are pointing to has a link to some other resource. It could be a simple navigation to a sub-page, the display of a full-screen image, or a link to an external site. The nature of a link is not revealed by the rollover. Rollovers can also have an intrinsic application that is often used on educational and promotional sites. Rolling over CD titles, for example, might reveal photographs of the CD sleeves, while rolling your mouse over a map of the world might Ilustrate each country or continent with a characteristic visual. Whether links are involved or not, the method of creating a rollover is the same.

Rollover events

Website designers use a host of identifiable effects for rollovers. Here are just a few.

Here's a selection of ways in which text can be changed to either acknowledge that a mouse is rolling over or the mouse button has been pressed.

1

2

3

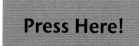

4

5

6

7

8

9

1|2 *The depressed button. Perhaps the most obvious and literal effect, this uses a pair of button images that switch depending on the position (or state) of the mouse.*

3 *Original: the appearance of the text with no mouse present.*

4 *Change in color.*

5 *Blurred text.*

6 *Black button.*

7 *Drop shadow.*

8 *Cloudy text.*

9 *Added colors.*

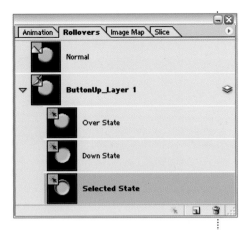

Here's the Rollover palette from ImageReady 7. Earlier versions use an alternative palette, but rollover states are created in much the same way. You can change the state of each by clicking on the heading and making a selection from the dropdown menu.

Rollover states

The six rollover states supported by ImageReady are listed and described below. You can display the options from the popup menu above the rollover thumbnail.

Over This is the rollover state set when the Web browser viewer rolls over with the mouse button up (i.e. not pressed).

Down Defines the rollover state when the mouse button is pressed over the rollover. The state is made visible for as long as the mouse button is pressed.

Click Defines the rollover state when the mouse is clicked over the rollover position. The state appears after the mouse is clicked and the button released.

Out Defines the rollover state when the mouse is moved out of the rollover position.

Up The mouse button, pressed and held prior to entering the rollover position is released inside.

Custom Enables the creation of a new, customized rollover state. (You will need to provide the appropriate code for this action.)

An additional state, *None*, preserves the current state of the image. This is in order that it can be used later as a rollover state. Bear in mind that when a rollover is assigned with this state it cannot be displayed on the webpage.

The Rollover palette

The Rollover palette is found only in ImageReady. It can be displayed (if not currently visible) by selecting *Window* > ***Show Rollover.***

The current image is displayed at the top of the palette with rollover states, if any, listed below.

You can create a new rollover state by clicking on the *New Rollover State* button at the base of the palette or, if you are creating a new rollover, by clicking on the alternate *Create Layer Based Rollover* button. Rollover states are automatically created in the sequence *Over, Down, Click, Selected*, and *Out* but each can be assigned an alternative state using the *Rollover State Options* palette. Click in the respective state to reveal the palette.

164 Creating your first rollover

You can create a rollover using a set of existing artwork, or start afresh. In this example we assume we have no previous material to use.

❶ Create a new image to form the basis of the rollover. You can do this in Photoshop or ImageReady, but since we will need to use ImageReady in the course of the project it makes sense to use this application from the outset. Type in some text. If you prefer to use graphics, add these to a new layer to enable layer effects and changes to be employed later. This will comprise our *Normal* rollover state.

❷ Arrange the desktop so that the *Optimize, Layers*, and *Rollover* palettes are visible. Use the *Window* menu to show any palettes not currently visible. Notice that our text has appeared as the first window in the *Rollover* palette. This is presented with a pale blue background, in a similar way to an active layer in the *Layers* menu. All obvious in this case, it is important to note later.

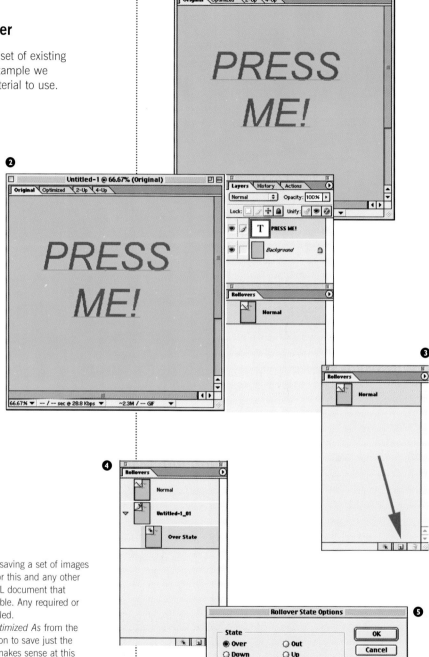

T I P

Saving your rollover

Saving your rollover involves saving a set of images corresponding to the states for this and any other rollovers, along with an HTML document that arranges all the files into a table. Any required or additional code is also compiled.

Save by selecting *Save Optimized As* from the *File* menu. You have the option to save just the HTML or images or both. It makes sense at this stage to save both. You can also save code for using with Adobe's GoLive website building software. You need only tick the box corresponding to this if you intend now, or in the near future, to use this application.

❻

❼

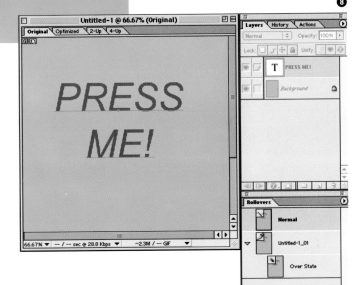

❽

❾

❸ Click the *New State* icon at the base of the *Rollovers* palette. This is indicated by a "paper sheet" icon.

❹ A new "level" has now appeared below the original to denote our current image slice. A second, representing the first new state (*Over*), has appeared beneath that. When created, the new state contains a thumbnail of the original image.

❺ We can change the state to that of a different mouse event by doubleclicking on the state to open the *Rollover State Options* menu. Make a new selection.

We can now create a graphic to represent the look we require. This could involve selecting a different image, or it could be a modification of the existing one. For this example, let's modify the original text. When the *Over* state is selected, any changes we make to the graphic (shown in the *Layers* palette) only affect this state.

❻ Apply a layer style (or a style) to the text with the *Over* state selected. Here we've used a simple drop shadow.

❼ Select the *Preview Document* button on the toolbar to preview the rollover.

❽❾ Now when you move your mouse from the desktop to the image space, you will see the rollover operate.

If you are happy with the rollover you could either proceed with further states (in exactly the same way) or else optimize and save your image.

166 Using existing images and graphics in a rollover

Earlier we produced two graphics of a button, *Button Up* and *Button Down*. Here's how to use those two images to construct a rollover. Remember that it is essential when using two images that both are identical in terms of their dimensions and resolution.

❶ Open the *Button Up* and *Button Down* images on the desktop and add a second rollover state for the *Button Up* image.

❷ Select the *Button Down* image. The *Rollover* palette will reset for this image. Create a new state for this image.

❸ Highlight the *Over* state thumbnail and click on the palette arrowhead to open the palette menu. Select *Copy Rollover State*.

❹ Select the *Button Up* image and click on the over state in the rollover palette for this image. Open the menu again and select *Paste Rollover State*. The second thumbnail will now show *Button Down* as a thumbnail.

Test the rollover by pressing the *Preview Document* button.

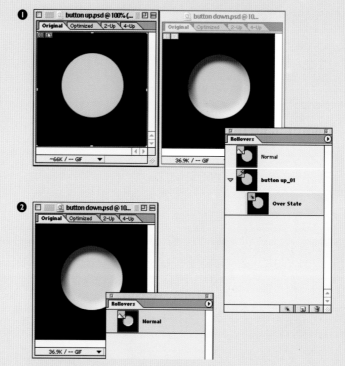

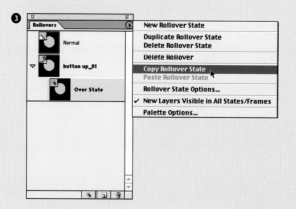

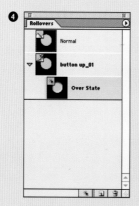

❺ Here we went on, by repeating the process, to add a third *Down* button that was created earlier using the *Contour* control. When the mouse button is pressed over the image, with *Preview Rollover* selected, this third state becomes active.

Given the constraints on size, any images, graphics, or mixture of the two can be used to build a rollover. When you optimize a rollover, the same optimization settings are applied throughout. If you have a graphic and image, both must be optimized as a GIF or JPEG.

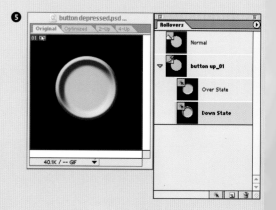

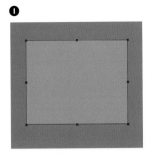

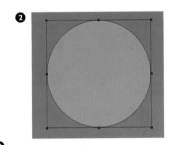

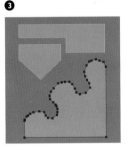

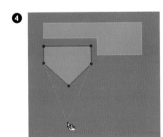

❶ The *Image Map* tools include tools for creating rectangles, circles, and, polygons, and a *Select* tool for selecting and modifying an existing image map.

❷ The *Rectangle* tool is ideal for drawing image maps that are principally square or rectangular in form.

❸ The *Circle* tool draws perfect circles. The shape and size can be modified later using the *Select* tool.

❹ Regular and irregular polygons can be drawn with the *Polygonal* tool. By using very short sides, curves can also be drawn.

❺ The *Image Map Select* tool enables an existing image map to be modified. In complex polygons you can also add and subtract points if you need to define an edge better.

❻ You can align the elements via the dropdown menu.

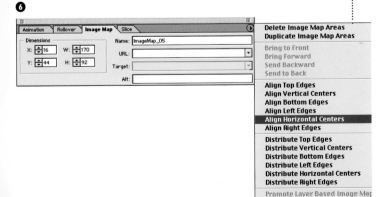

IMAGE MAPS

Image maps are HTML codes that define areas of an image and enable them to act as links. Such areas are colloquially known as "hotspots". Although the graphics for an image map can be created in Photoshop or Elements, you need ImageReady to create a working image map.

When you roll over an image map the mouse pointer will change to the hand pointer icon and, should you click on this region, will take you to the corresponding page. Image maps are useful where the website designer would like active areas to be determined by the shape of the underlying graphics (or image) rather than having to accommodate the limitations imposed by image slices.

Here is an example of how image maps can be effectively used. You have a website relating to your hometown or village. Your homepage is an aerial view of the town, and you can use image maps to define principal buildings. Then, when a visitor clicks on the school or community center they can be linked to pages relating to these facilities.

Image map tools

ImageReady features a set of tools for creating image maps. You can also use the contents of a layer to define the extent of an image map.

Image maps created using these are known as tool-based image maps and can be made up of a rectangular, circle, or polygonal. The *Polygonal* tool covers almost any shape as it can be used rather like a selection tool to define the boundary of the map. The more sides you choose to give the polygon the smoother the shape will ultimately be.

Layer-based image maps are constructed from the nontransparent pixels in an image layer. You can use the *Image Map* tools to define an area smaller than that of the nontransparent pixels, as long as your shape fits within those areas.

Image map palette

The Image Map palette can be displayed by selecting *Window > **Show Image Map*** or by clicking on the *Image Map* tab in the *Rollover* palette.

168 Creating an image map

1 Your choice of tool will be determined by the shape you need to define. In this graphic there are some simple as well as compound shapes that need defining.

2 Begin by defining one of the blue globes. Select the *Circular Image Map* tool and drag it over the globe.

3 If the shape is too large, small, or imprecisely aligned, use the *Image Map Select* tool to resize or reposition it.

4 An irregular area can be selected by using the *Polygonal* tool. You can use the *Image Map Select* tool again if this shape needs refining further.

5 For each image map, open the *Image Map* palette and enter an absolute or relative URL for the required link.

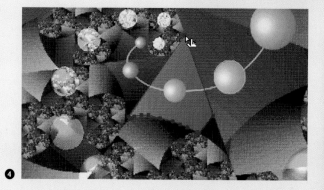

Image map rollovers

You can create rollover effects for image maps in a similar way to those you created for image slices. Note that, although the area defined for the rollover is the image map, rollovers will only transpose images in a slice. If the image is not sliced, then any layer changes will take place on the auto-slice (that is, the whole image), which may not be the effect you require. Therefore, you should ensure that your image is sliced beforehand.

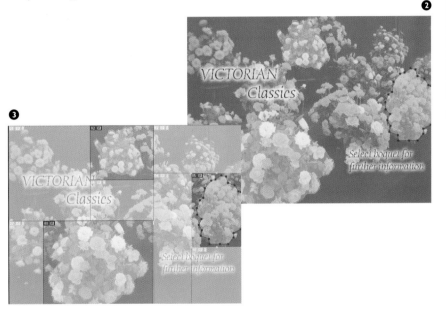

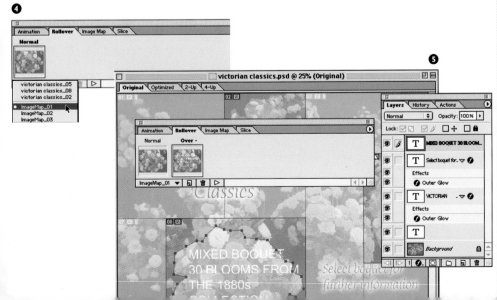

❶ We'll use this page from the "Victorian Classics" website. The aim is that a visitor will click on a bouquet and find out further information.

❷ Create an image map, or maps, on a chosen image.

❸ If it is important that a restricted area of the image is affected by the rollover, add image slices and position them appropriately over the image map areas.

❹ Open the *Rollover* palette (if it is not currently displayed). Open the menu at the bottom left-hand corner and select the appropriate image map. If you have not named the image maps, they will be numbered systematically in the order of creation. In this case the image slices (user-slices) are also numbered.

Click on the *New Rollover State* icon and select the required state from the dropdown menu above the new thumbnail.

❺ Using the *Layers* palette (as for conventional rollovers) modify the image for the new state. Try adding a new text layer that will appear in the *Mouse Over* state. This layer is turned off for the normal state.

Test your rollover in the usual way, using the *Rollover Preview* button, or *Preview in Browser* button. Repeat the process for any other image maps.

Although this situation features both image maps and slices, the rollover is only activated when the mouse rolls over the area defined by the image map.

170   More about image maps

Saving Image Maps

It is important, when saving an image containing image maps, to also save the HTML document, because this document contains the image map information and definition. Also, in the *Output Settings* dialog (*File > Save Optimized As > Output Settings*) ensure that the *Image Map Type* is set to *Client Side*. This hands over the responsibility of image map management to the user's browser.

Alignment and Distribution

Multiple image maps within an image can be aligned and distributed in the same way as slices. This is more useful when using image maps as the basis for a design, rather than using the image maps to define existing areas. The align and distribution tools can be found in the *Image Map* pullout menu and on the *Tool Options* bar.

Overlapping Image Maps

It is possible to create image maps that overlap others. The link that is activated when a mouse is clicked on an overlap area is determined by the stacking order. Normally, image maps are stacked (in the manner of image layers) over each other in the order of creation. Where there is an overlap, the uppermost image map has precedence and its link is used.

You can use the buttons on the *Tool Options* bar (or the commands in the *Image Map* palette menu) to rearrange selected items. After selecting an image map you can *Bring to Front, Bring Forward* (that is, raise it one "layer"), *Send to Back* or *Send Backward* (back one "layer").

❶ The *Image Map* tool (featuring options for rectangular, circular, and polygonal image maps, and the *Image Map Select* tool) is detachable and can be placed anywhere in the workspace.

❷ The *Tool Options* palette offers alignment and distribution tools.

❸ You can select one or all the image maps on an image by using the *Image Map Select* tool. Drag the tool (in the same manner as the *Marquee* tool) across those image maps that you wish to include.

❹ You can use the alignment and distribution tools to arrange selected maps.

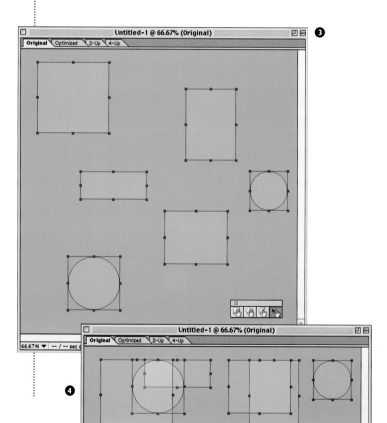

❺

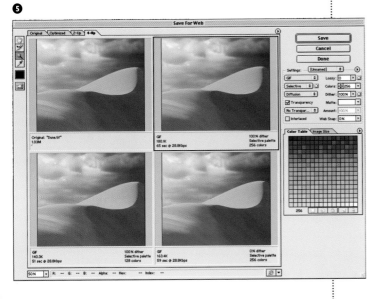

Saving optimized images with Web elements

We've discussed three principal options for saving optimized images throughout this book. Now, in the light of exploring more Web elements it seems appropriate to revisit the options that are available:

- *HTML and Images*
- *Images Only*
- *HTML Only*

Saving optimized images as *HTML and Images* generates all the files needed for using the image on a website. For a sliced image, all the separate image files and the HTML file are created along with any special effects, such as the inclusion of links to other pages, rollovers, and image maps. If there are GIF animations involved, these are included too. This would normally be the best option to choose when creating elements that are destined for the Web.

Images Only will save your image in the format specified in the *Optimization* palette (or elsewhere). Sliced images will be saved as a set of files.

HTML Only saves the HTML code generated for your images and Web elements. You can create an HTML file in ImageReady using the *Copy HTML* command, which will be separate from your original images and the HTML for those images.

Left is the basic process that you need to follow to save optimized images.

❻

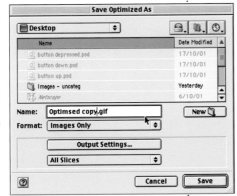

❼

❺ In Photoshop only select *File > Save for Web*.

❻ Apply optimization settings. (These were discussed from page 94 onwards.)

❼ Click *OK* in the Save for Web dialog box in Photoshop or select *File > Save Optimized* in ImageReady (this will save the file in the current state). Use the alternative *Save Optimized As* to save a new copy so that you do not overwrite any settings that were made when the file was previously saved.

❽ Give a filename and location then enter in the *Format* option one of these three options: *HTML and Images*, *Images Only*, or *HTML Only*.

❾ If appropriate, select a slices option from the popup menu. This can be *All Slices*, to save all the slices in an image, or *Selected Slices*. In the latter case, where the selected slices comprise only a small part of the image, HTML is generated only for the box bounded by the outer edges of the selected slices. Appropriate auto-slices are generated to fill the intervening space. Click *Save*.

❽

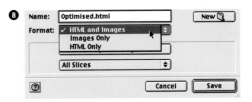

❾

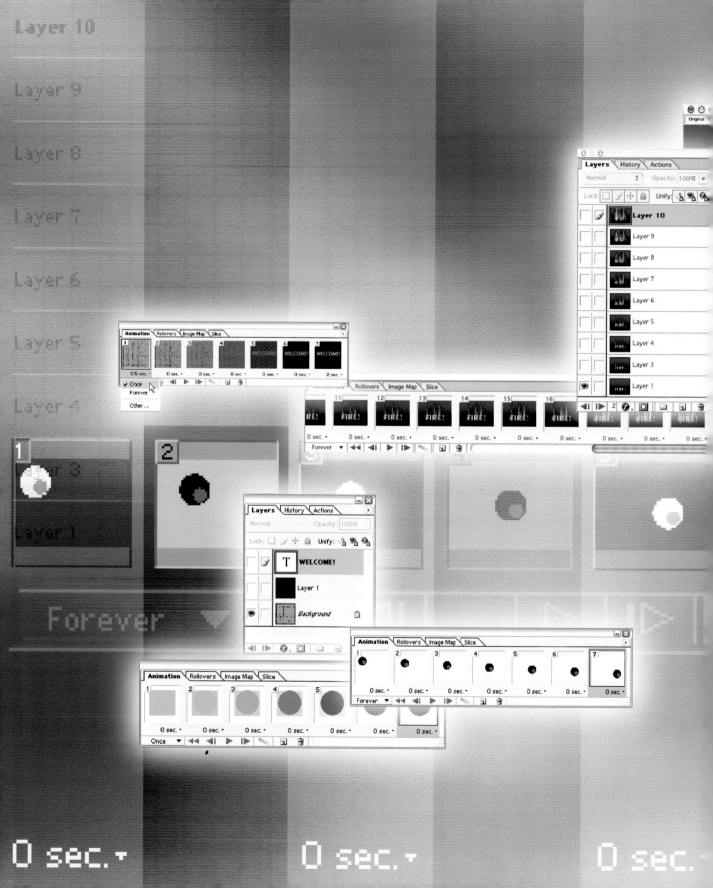

mation.psd @ 100% (Original)

▼ -2.2M / -- GIF   ▼

C H A P T E R **7**

Animation

Animation processes are similar to
those we've discussed with regard
to slices and rollovers. The Animation
palette (in ImageReady only) bears a
particularly close resemblance to that
of rollovers, and if you are already
comfortable creating rollovers,
animations should be easy.

0 sec. ▼   0 sec. ▼

AN INTRODUCTION TO ANIMATION

Animation—the traditional type expounded by the likes of Disney—involves the laborious action of drawing and painting individual cells for each of the 25 image frames that compose every single second of film. The recent advances in computer-generated imaging aside, the process of showing these drawings in quick succession gives the impression of movement and life.

Animation, or more precisely GIF Animation, uses many similar principles—the GIF file format alone has the capacity to display multiple frames sequentially. A GIF Animation sequence, when configured with consecutive images, delivers an animation if played in a Web browser. The nature of the GIF format means there are certain restraints. You can only use a maximum of 256 colors and graphics containing large areas of flat color are preferred. However, these constraints should not limit the usefulness of the feature.

Using animations

The use of animation as a design element has been widespread. There was a time when no self-respecting corporate website would be without a rotating version of its company logo. Flash and Shockwave technology has eclipsed the use of GIF Animations on many of these sites, and it would be reasonable to question whether GIF Animation is likely to succumb to these superior technologies.

While there is no doubting that both Flash and Shockwave offer extensive opportunities to add dynamic events to a website, it's important to remember that GIF Animations are, by comparison, small files and they do not require additional plug-ins in order to function. A Web browser will, therefore, handle a GIF Animation as easily and transparently as a rollover. And GIF Animations are extremely easy to create!

1

2

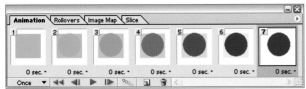

3

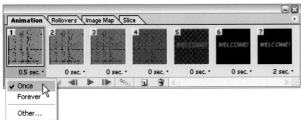

4

5

| New Frame |
| Delete Frame |
| Delete Animation |
| Copy Frame |
| Paste Frame... |
| Select All Frames |
| Tween... |
| Reverse Frames |
| Optimize Animation... |
| Make Frames From Layers |
| Flatten Frames Into Layers |
| Create Layer for Each New Frame |
| ✔ New Layers Visible in All States/Frames |
| Palette Options... |

1 *The sequence of flaming text that you created using Eye Candy's Fire filter is a good example of manual animation creation.*

2 *Starting with a square and ending with a circle, the* Tween *command has been invoked to provide five intermediate frames to give a smooth transition from one to the other.*

3 Animation *palette*

4 Layers *palette*

5 *The* Animation *palette menu also provides access to additional functions such as optimizing and inter-frame manipulations.*

Animation engineering

The animation process (we'll simply use the term 'animation' rather than 'GIF Animation' from now on) comes in two varieties. The simplest involves a process known a tweening. This analyzes both a start and an end image that you provide, and then adds additional intermediate images to provide a smooth transition between the two. The process is a little like morphing, but while morphing can transform one object into another, entirely different one, tweening can only provide simple staged transformations. These might be shape-based, positional, or layer-based.

The second process, often regarded as more long-winded, is to create each frame individually. This results in more controlled animations, but you need to be careful to ensure that consecutive frames lead on from one another in a logical and—in animation terms—flowing manner.

Another term likely to be unfamiliar to anyone who has not encountered animations before is *Frame Disposal*. This command determines how frames of animation follow each other.

The animation palette

The Animation palette (displayed by selecting *Window* > *Show Animation*, or by clicking on the *Animation* tab on the *Rollover* palette) has a layout similar to that of the *Rollover* palette. The animation is shown as a series of thumbnails.

Animation Frames

Frame Delay A user-definable duration for each frame in the animation to be displayed.
Looping control Gives the option of playing the animation continuously, once only, or a specified number of times.
Playback controls From left to right, *Select First Frame, Select Previous Frame, Stop, Play, Select Next Frame.*
Tweening button Press to open the *Tween* dialog.
Add Frame Button (*Layers* palette) Changes frames forward or backward. Frames can be reordered in the timeline by dragging and dropping from old to new locations.

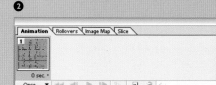

176 CREATING YOUR FIRST ANIMATION

Use the tween method to create a simple—but effective—welcome message for a webpage. This will appear out of the background of that webpage.

1 Open a new document that will comprise your first frame and fill it with the same color and/or texture as the webpage. (If you'd just like to practice the technique and haven't yet created your webpage don't worry. Just fill a new document with a color.) To create a compact animation, don't make it any more than around 300 pixels square.

2 Open both the *Animation* and *Layers* palettes. Your graphic will appear in the first window of the *Animation* palette and as *Layer 0* in the *Layers* palette.

3 Create the last frame of the animation. Add a new layer to the original image and fill this with black. Add a type layer by typing in a "welcome" notice.

4 Click on the *New Frame* button on the *Animation* palette to add a new frame. With this highlighted (shown by its black frame), check the thumbnail is showing your welcome note.

5 Click on the first thumbnail to highlight this. Now, on the *Layers* palette, click on the "eye" icon next to the black-filled layer and the type layer to turn these off. The thumbnail should now display the original color.

6 Click on the *Tween* button to open the *Tween* dialog. Select the default number of frames (five) and press the *All Layers* radio button.

7 Click *OK* and the new frames will be added to the *Animation* palette. If you press the *Play* button now you'll see them scroll through (somewhat jerkily) on the original image window.

Now set the display time for each frame. Give the first a time of one second—the others can be left at zero. Because the animation will be playing only once the final frame will remain on screen indefinitely. (If this were not the case you might want to add a delay of a few seconds to this frame prior to the animation looping back the first.) Click on the time under each thumbnail to reveal the timing options.

To play the animation just once select Once from the dropdown menu (in the bottom left of *Animation* palette). Then hit the *Play* button. Your animation is ready to go. As with other Web effects it often better to preview the effect in a browser. this will give you a better indication of how the animation will work when it is downloaded.

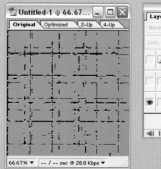

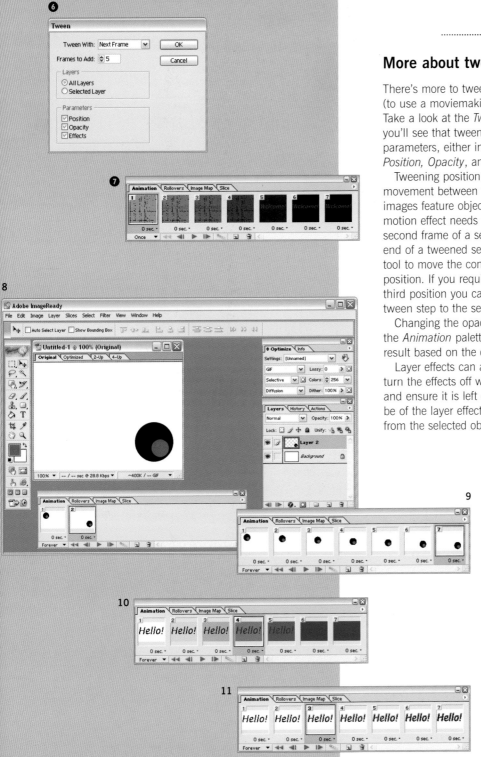

More about tweening

There's more to tweening than the simple crossfade (to use a moviemaking term) that you've used here. Take a look at the *Tween* command dialog box and you'll see that tweening can be effected by three parameters, either individually or in combination: *Position, Opacity*, and *Effects*.

Tweening position will produce a steady movement between frames where the first and last images feature objects in different positions. The motion effect needs to be generated by selecting the second frame of a sequence (i.e., that forming the end of a tweened sequence) and using the *Move* tool to move the contents of the layer to a new position. If you require the object to pass through a third position you can do so by adding a second tween step to the sequence.

Changing the opacity in the second window of the *Animation* palette will similarly give a tweened result based on the change in opacity.

Layer effects can also be tweened. To do this, turn the effects off when one thumbnail is selected, and ensure it is left on for the other. The effect will be of the layer effect appearing (or disappearing) from the selected objects.

8|9 *For this positional tween, the ball was dragged to the lower right corner when the second thumbnail was active. Then the* Tween *command was applied with the* Position *parameter selected.*

10 *By setting the opacity to 0 percent in one frame and to 100 percent in the other, the result is a gradual fading of the layer to allow the text to appear (or, in this case, disappear).*

11 *A chiseled* Pillow Emboss *layer style has been applied to the second thumbnail, but turned off for the first. The tweened result shows the effect building up toward the end of the sequence.*

178   Frame disposal

A hidden feature of animations, which is available
due to the GIF file format's support of transparency,
is frame disposal. For each frame of your animation
you can set a frame disposal method that
determines whether or not the image contained in
a frame is removed when the next frame is loaded.
You can see the *Disposal Method* options by
selecting a frame and then right clicking (in
Windows) or Apple clicking (in Mac OS). The
options are *Automatic* (the default setting, which is
appropriate for most animations), *Do not Dispose*
and *Restore to Background*.

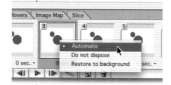

If you select *Do not Dispose* the current frame
will remain onscreen when the next is displayed
and will also show through any transparent areas
in that new frame. *Restore to Background* removes
the current frame when the next appears, but
enables the background color to show through in
any transparent areas. A typical example of this
might be to let an animated object appear to move
over the surface of the webpage. Note that the
frame disposal method cannot be previewed in
ImageReady; you'll have to use *Preview* in your
Web browser to check that any disposal method
has the intended result.

Creating an animation using multiple frames

The *Tween* command, as you can see, is adept at
making very smooth and effective transitions
between two images. Had the animation been more
ambitious then it would have been equally effective
at adding further transitions.

The alternative method of animation involving
multiple frames, where several original and
intermediate images are used in place of those
automatically generated by the *Tween* command,
would seem redundant. While it is true that
tweening produces smoother transitions than you
might achieve manually, in these circumstances
there will be times when the more considered
approach of multiple original image is more
effective. In the "Fire" example, you are not dealing
with such smooth transitions and there is an
element of randomness in the growth of the flames.

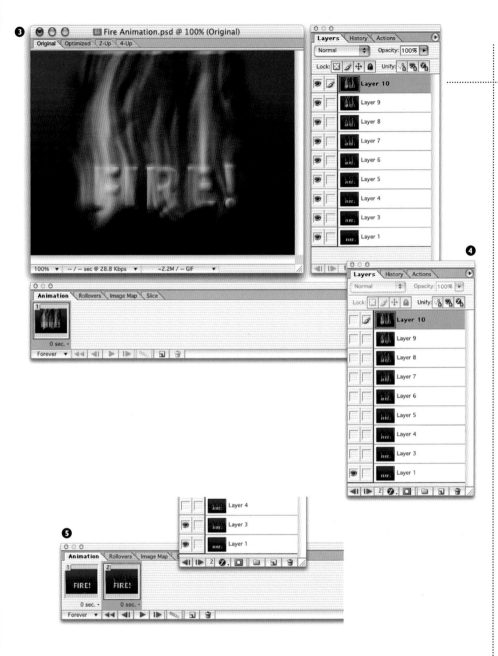

❶ Open the original image which is the text without any flame embellishment. Make sure the *Animation* and *Layers* palettes are also open.

❷ Create a new, empty layer in this image by selecting *Layer > New > **Layer***. Open the next image in the sequence, select (*Select > **All***) and copy (*Edit > **Copy***) the entire image and then paste it into the new layer.

❸ Continue adding new layers and pasting successive images into them.

❹ When the sequence is complete, turn your attention to the *Animation* and *Layers* palettes. There is currently only one thumbnail visible and it will be of the last image put into the *Layers* palette (that is, the uppermost layer). Click on all the *Layer Visibility* ("eye") icons in the *Layers* palettes to turn them off, apart from the lowermost layer.

❺ Add a new animation frame by clicking on the *New Frame* icon. Click on the eye icon above the lowermost layer to turn it on again.

Continue adding new frames and turning on the next highest layer for each.

When complete, play the animation.

❻ If, despite your best efforts, the animation plays a little roughly (because the transitions between frames are a little abrupt) you can still use the *Tween* command to insert additional frames between existing pairs. This time, one, or perhaps two, would be appropriate to add.

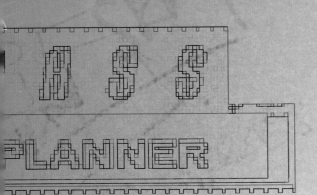

Reference

Glossary

Editor's Note: Due to the enormous number of features, tools and filters in Adobe Photoshop and ImageReady, this glossary is limited to general terms used throughout the book. For information on specific tools and features, please refer to the Index and turn to the relevant page or chapter.

8-bit Of display monitors or digital images—the allocation of eight data bits to each pixel, producing a display or image of 256 grays or colors.

24-bit As above, the allocation of 24 bits of memory to each pixel, giving a possible screen display of 16.7 million colors. Twenty-four bits are required for CMYK separations—eight bits for each.

additive colors The color model describing the colors of transmitted light: red, green, and blue (RGB).

alpha channel In Photoshop, a separate channel where information regarding the transparency of a pixel is kept. "Masks" are also stored here, simulating the physical material used in platemaking to shield parts of the plate from light. The alpha channel is additional to the three RGB or four CMYK channels.

animated GIF A GIF file containing several GIF images, which, when displayed in turn, produce an animation. The delay between frames and the number of times the animation should loop can be specified in the file.

animation The process of creating a moving image, usually by rapidly moving from one still image to the next.

antialias/antialiasing A technique of optically eliminating the jagged effect of bitmapped images or text, as reproduced on low-resolution devices such as monitors. This is achieved by adding pixels of an in-between tone—the edges of the object's color are blended with its background by averaging the density of the range of pixels involved.

artifact A visible flaw in an electronically prepared image, usually as a result of the imaging technique employed, such as in JPEG compression, for example.

background The area of an image on which the principal subject or foreground sits. It may be colored to give extra definition to the image.

banner A graphic image used on a website as a header or, more often, as an advertisement. Banners can be a simple graphic or can contain animation and even **rich media**.

bas relief An image that is embossed and stands out in shallow relief from a flat background, designed to give the illusion of further depth.

bevel A chamfered edge applied to type, buttons, or selections to emphasize a three-dimensional effect.

Bézier curve A curve whose shape is defined by a pair of "direction lines" at each end, which specify the direction and rate at which the curve leaves or enters the corresponding end point.

bilevel, bileveled Black-and-white images containing no intermediate grays.

binary A number system with the base 2, thus all values are expressed as combinations of 1 and 0. These correspond to states, which can be represented in computers as on/off or circuit closed/circuit open etc.

bit A contraction of "binary digit", the smallest piece of information a computer can use. A bit is expressed as one of two values, 1 or 0.

bit depth The number of bits assigned to each pixel on a monitor, scanner, or in an image file.

bitmap An array of values specifying the color of every pixel in a digital image.

bitmapped graphic An image made up of dots, or pixels, as distinct from the vector images created by object-oriented drawing applications.

blend(ing) The merging of two or more colors, forming a graduated transition from one to the other. The quality of the blend is limited by the number of shades of a single color that can be reproduced without visible "banding."

brightness The amount of light reflected by a color.

browser Program that enables the viewing or "browsing" of World Wide Web pages across the Internet. Popular browers include Explorer, Navigator, and Opera.

calibrate, calibration The process of adjusting a machine or piece of hardware to conform to a known scale or standard so that it performs more accurately.

capture The action of "getting" an image, by taking a photograph, scanning an image into a computer, or "grabbing" an image using a frame grabber.

centered Type that is centered in its measure, as distinct from type that is ranged (aligned) left, right, or "justified" (ranged across the complete type measure).

chroma The intensity, or purity, of a color; thus its degree of saturation.

clip art / clip media Collections of (usually) royalty-free photographs, illustrations, design devices, and other precreated items, such as sounds. These often come bundled with popular software packages.

clipping Limiting an image within the bounds of a given area.

CMYK Cyan, magenta, yellow, and key plate (black). The four printing-process colors based on the subtractive color model (black is represented by the letter K, for "key plate," the plate which carries the black).

collage An image assembled from elements drawn from different sources. Also known as a montage or (for photographic subjects) photomontage.

color cast A bias in a color image that can be either intentional or undesirable.

color gamut, color space Describes the full range of colors achievable by any single device on the reproduction chain. For example, the 16.7 million colors that can be displayed on current monitors cannot be printed on a commercial four-color press. For this reason, various color-management systems (CMS) have been devised to maintain the consistency of color gamuts across various devices.

color picker A color model displayed on a computer monitor. Color pickers may be specific to an application, such as

Photoshop, to a third-party color model such as PANTONE®, or to the operating system of your computer.

compression The technique of rearranging data so that it either occupies less space on disk or transfers faster between devices, or on communication lines. Compression methods that do not lose data are referred to as "lossless," while "lossy" is used to describe methods in which some data is lost. Movies and animations employ techniques called "codecs" (compression/decompression).

constrain A facility in some applications to contain one or more items within another.

contrast The degree of difference between adjacent tones in an image (or on a computer monitor) from the lightest to the darkest. "High contrast" describes an image with light highlights and dark shadows, but with few shades in between, while a "low contrast" image is one with even tones and few dark areas or highlights.

copyright The right of a person who creates an original work to protect that work by controlling how and where it may be reproduced. Ownership of the work does not automatically signify ownership of copyright (and vice versa).

copyright-free A misnomer used to describe ready-made resources such as clip art. Resources described as such are rarely, if ever, "copyright free." The correct description is normally "royalty free."

crop To trim or mask an image so that it fits a given area, or to discard unwanted portions of an image.

cyan With magenta and yellow, one of the three subtractive primaries and one of the three process colors used in four-color printing. Sometimes referred to as **process blue**.

definition The overall quality—or clarity—of an image, determined by the combined, subjective effect of graininess (or resolution in a digital image) and sharpness.

density The darkness of tone or color in any image. In a transparency this refers to the amount of light which can pass through it, thus determining the darkness of shadows and the saturation of color.

density range The maximum range of tones in an image,

184 measured as the difference between the maximum and minimum densities (the darkest and lightest tones).

diffuser Any material that scatters transmitted light, thus increasing the area of the light source.

digital photography The process of either capturing an image with digital equipment or manipulating photographic images on a computer, or both. Images are thus captured and/or manipulated in binary form, rather than on film.

digitize To convert anything, for example text, images, or sound, into binary form so that it can be digitally processed, manipulated, stored, and reconstructed.

dither(ed), dithering The use of patterns of pixels of available colors, for example, the colors in a Web-safe palette, to simulate missing colors, based on the principle of optical mixing. Dithered images often have a "dotty" appearance when closely inspected.

dots per inch (dpi) A unit of measurement used to represent the resolution of devices such as printers and imagesetters and, increasingly, monitors and images, whose resolution should more properly be expressed in pixels per inch (ppi). The closer the dots or pixels (the more there are to each inch) the better the quality. Typical resolutions are 72 ppi for a monitor, 600 dpi for a laser printer, and 2450 dpi (or more) for an imagesetter.

drop shadow A shadow projected onto the background behind an image or character, designed to lift the image or character off the surface.

dynamic HTML/DHTML Dynamic Hypertext Markup Language. A development of the basic HTML code used to create webpages that enables users to add enhanced features, such as basic animations and highlighted buttons without relying on browser plug-ins. DHTML compatibility is built into later versions (version 4.0 onwards) of browsers.

dynamic range In electronic imaging, the range of light levels recordable by a CCD (charge-coupled device) or other electronic imaging device.

EPS (encapsulated PostScript) A standard graphics file format used primarily for storing object-oriented (or "vector") graphics files generated by drawing applications, such as

Adobe Illustrator and Macromedia FreeHand. An EPS file usually has two parts: one containing the PostScript code that tells the printer how to print the image, the other an onscreen preview, which can be a PICT, TIFF, or JPEG.

export A feature provided by many applications allowing you to save a file in a format so that it can be used by another application, or a different operating system. For example, an illustration created in a drawing application may be exported as an EPS file so that it can be used in a page-layout application, such as QuarkXPress.

Extensible Hypertext Markup Language (XHTML) A blend of the features of **XML** and **HTML**. XHTML is platform independent.

Extensible Markup Language (XML) A possible ultimate successor to HTML offering more sophisticated control and formatting options.

eyedropper tool A tool for gauging and sampling the color of adjacent pixels.

face Traditionally the printing surface of any metal type character, but nowadays used as a series or family name for fonts with similar characteristics, such as "modern face" or "old face."

filter A filter can be any component that provides the basic building blocks for processing data. However, the term is more commonly used to describe particular functions within an application. In Photoshop, it refers to the numerous functions that apply special visual effects to images, borrowing the term from the colored-glass, tinted-gelatin, or cellulose-acetate sheets used in conventional color separation, and the lens-mounted filters used in conventional and digital photography.

File Transfer Protocol (FTP) A standard system for transmitting files between computers. Although Web browsers incorporate FTP capabilities, dedicated FTP applications provide greater flexibility. Typically, when creating a webpage, an FTP application will be used to upload this to the Web.

font A set of characters sharing the same typeface and size.

font family The complete set of characters of a typeface design in all its sizes and styles. A typical font family contains four individual fonts: roman, italic, bold and bold italic. Also known as a "type family."

fractal Infinitely variable shapes defined by complex but precise mathematical expressions. Some Photoshop filters (notably Kai's Power Tools) make extensive use of fractals, allowing users to make bold graphics from scratch and use image elements as the basic component.

frame A single still picture from a movie or animation sequence. Also a single complete image from a TV picture (which normally comprises two interlaced fields, each carrying alternate line information).

frame grab(bing) The capture of a single still frame from a video sequence.

gamma A measure of contrast in a digital image, or in a photographic film, paper, or processing technique.

gamma correction Modification of the midtones of an image by compressing or expanding the range, thus altering the contrast. Also known as **tone correction**.

gamut compression Gamut mapping where the range of color values produced by an input device is compressed to fit the smaller gamut of an output device. Gamut compression can be crucial to good color reproduction, but colors that have been gamut compressed will seldom match the original.

GIF Graphics Interchange Format. One of the main bitmapped image formats used on the Internet. GIF is a 256-color format with two specifications, GIF87a and, more recently, GIF89a, the latter providing additional features such as transparent backgrounds. The GIF format uses a "lossless" compression technique, or "algorithm," and thus does not squeeze files as much as the JPEG format, which is "lossy" (some data is discarded). For use in Web browsers JPEG is the format of choice for tone images, such as photographs, while GIF is more suitable for line images and other graphics, such as text.

graduation / gradation The smooth transition from one color or tone to another.

graphic A general term describing any illustration or drawn design.

grayscale The rendering of an image in a range of grays from white to black. In a digital image or on a computer monitor, this usually means that an image is rendered with eight bits assigned to each pixel, giving a maximum of 256 levels of gray.

hex(adecimal) The use of the number 16 as the basis of a counting system, as distinct from our conventional decimal (base ten) system or the binary (base two) system used by basic computer processes (see previous spread). The figures are represented by the numbers 1 to 9, followed by the letters A to F. Thus decimal 9 is still hex 9, while decimal 10 becomes hex A, decimal 16 becomes hex 10, decimal 26 becomes hex 1A, and so on.

HSL Hue, Saturation, Lightness. A color model based upon the light transmitted either in an image or in your monitor—hue being the spectral color (the actual pigment color), saturation being the intensity of the color pigment (without black or white added), and brightness representing the strength of luminance from light to dark (the amount of black or white present).

hue Pure spectral color, which distinguishes a color from others. Red is a different hue from blue; and although light red and dark red may contain varying amounts of white or black, they may be the same hue.

Hypertext Markup Language (HTML) A text-based "page description language" (PDL) used to format documents published on the World Wide Web, and which can be viewed with Web browsers. Many webpage creation tools help create pages by using "WYSIWYG" displays, in which page elements are positioned by the user and text added appropriately. Such creations are converted to HTML before the website is posted to its ultimate location.

icon A graphical representation of an object (such as a disk, file, folder, or tool), used to make identification and selection easier. In most cases an icon can be clicked on to activate the function, object or software application it represents.

image area In Photoshop, the description of the area in a program interface where the image to be manipulated sits.

image library A source of original transparencies and pictures that can be used for virtually any purpose on payment of a fee. This usually varies according to usage

—a picture to be used in an advertisement will invariably cost a great deal more than the same picture for use in a school textbook. Many libraries specialize in various subjects, such as garden plants, wildlife, and fine art.

palette Refers to a subset of colors that are needed to display a particular image. For instance, a GIF image will have a palette containing a maximum of 256 individual and distinct colors.

image map An image that features a set of embedded links to other documents or websites. These are activated when the mouse is clicked on the appropriate area. Often the "front page" of a website contains such a map. Similar functions can be created by slicing an image into sections.

image resource A source of ready-made material such as royalty-free image libraries, clip art, and mapping resources distributed digitally on various media such as CD-ROM and the Web. Distinct from "image libraries," which supply original transparencies and pictures.

image size A description of the dimensions of an image. Depending on the type of image being measured, this can be in terms of linear dimensions, resolution, or digital file size.

image slicing The practice of dividing a digital image into rectangular areas or slices, to each of which can be added an active link or other function. However, the image appears as a single entity when viewed on a website, as the individual slices remain invisible to the viewer.

imaging device A general term describing any dedicated piece of equipment that either captures an image from an original, such as a scanner or camera, or generates an image from a previously captured original, such as a contact printing frame or imagesetter.

import To bring text, pictures, or other data into a document.

interlacing A technique of displaying an image on a Web page so that the image reveals increasing detail as it downloads. Interlacing is usually offered as an option when saving images in GIF, PNG, and JPEG ("progressive") formats in Photoshop.

Internet The world-wide network of computers linked by telephone (or other connections), providing individual and corporate users with access to information, companies, newsgroups, discussion areas, and much more.

Internet Explorer / Explorer A cross-platform Web browser produced by Microsoft.

Internet service provider (ISP) Any organization that provides access to the Internet. Often this is a gateway to the Internet (giving users access to both webpages and email), but many ISPs also provide additional services (such as information and shopping pages) and space for the user to create their own webpages.

interpolation A computer calculation used to estimate unknown values that fall between known ones. One use of this process is to redefine pixels in bitmapped images after they have been modified, for instance, when an image is resized ("resampled") or rotated. In such cases the program takes estimates from the known values of other pixels lying in the same or similar ranges. Interpolation is also used by some scanning and image-manipulation software to enhance the resolution of images that have been scanned at low resolution. Photoshop offers Nearest Neighbor (for fast but imprecise results, which may produce jagged effects), Bilinear (for medium-quality results), and Bicubic (for smooth and precise results, but with slower performance).

ISO/Adobe character set The industry-standard character set for PostScript type faces. Access to characters depends on which operating system and application is being used

JPEG/JPG (Joint Photographic Experts Group) An ISO group that defines compression standards for bitmapped color images. The abbreviated form (pronounced "*jay-peg*") gives its name to a lossy, compressed file format in which the degree of compression from high compression/low quality to low compression/high quality can be defined by the user. It is particularly suitable for photographic images that are to be viewed in Web browsers.

landscape format An image or page format in which the width is greater than the height.

layer In Photoshop, a level to which you can consign an element of the design you are working on. Selected layers may be active (meaning you can work on them) or inactive. Some applications may not provide a layering feature, but nonetheless may lay items one on top of another in the order that you create them—and in some cases will allow you to send items to the back, or bring them to the front.

link A text element in an HTML document that takes the user to another location, page, or screen when clicked on.

light sensitive Any material or device that responds either chemically or digitally to light striking it, such as a photographic emulsion, or photosites on a digital camera.

lossless compression Methods of file compression in which no data is lost (as opposed to lossy compression).

lossy compression Methods of file compression in which some data may be irretrievably lost during compression (as opposed to lossless compression).

magenta With cyan and yellow, one of the three subtractive primaries, and one of the three process colors used in four-color printing. Sometimes called **process red**.

midtones/middletones The range of tonal values in an image anywhere between the darkest and lightest, usually referring to those approximately halfway.

moiré An unintended pattern that occurs in halftone reproduction when two or more colors are printed and the dot screens are positioned at the wrong angles. The correct angles at which screens should be positioned depends on the number of colors being printed, but the normal angles for four-color process printing, and thus the default setting in many computer applications, are: cyan 105°; magenta 75°; yellow 90°; black 45°. A moiré pattern can also be caused by scanning or rescreening an image to which a halftone screen has already been applied, such as in a magazine.

monitor Your computer screen, or the unit that houses it. Although most monitors use cathode-ray tubes, some contain liquid-crystal displays (LCDs)—particularly portables and laptops—and, more recently, gas plasma (large matrices of tiny, gas-filled glass cells).

mono(chrome) / monochromatic An image of varying tones reproduced in a single color.

Motion Picture Experts Group (MPEG) A compression format for squeezing full-screen, digital video files and animations, providing huge compression ratios.

mottling Image artifacts that can appear when an image containing large areas of flat color, or gentle gradients, is sharpened. The sharpening algorithm adds perceived detail but also acts on small fluctuations in these areas and accentuates them. JPEGs are particularly vulnerable.

multimedia Any combination of various digital media, such as sound, video, animation, graphics, and text, incorporated into a software product or presentation.

Navigator / Netscape A cross-platform Web browser produced by Netscape. Webpages should be checked in all the main browsers, as they may display differently.

operating system The software (and in some cases "firmware") that provides the environment within which all other software and its user operates. The major operating systems are Microsoft's "DOS" and "Windows," Apple's "Mac OS" and AT&T's "UNIX," the last three of which all use "GUIs" (graphical user interfaces). Mac OS X is Unix based.

optimization The process largely (but not exclusively) involving file compression, that makes a file more effective (in terms of size and speed of delivery) for Internet delivery.

orientation The print direction of a page, or format of an image (portrait or landscape).

origin The fixed or zero point of horizontal and vertical axes, or of the rulers featured in Photoshop (and most applications) from which measurements can be made.

PANTONE® The registered trademark of Pantone Inc.'s system of color standards and control and quality requirements, in which each color bears a description of its formulation (in percentages) for subsequent printing. The PANTONE MATCHING SYSTEM® is used throughout the world—consequently, colors specified by any designer can be matched exactly by any printer.

perspective A technique of rendering three-dimensional objects on a two-dimensional plane, duplicating the "real world" view by giving the same impression of the object's relative position and size when viewed from a particular point. The shorter the distance, the wider the perspective; the greater the distance, the narrower the perspective.

pixel Abbreviation for "picture element." The smallest

188 component of any digitally generated image, including text, such as a single dot of light on a computer screen. In its simplest form, one pixel corresponds to a single bit: 0 = off, or white; and 1 = on, or black. In color or grayscale images or monitors, one pixel may correspond to up to several bits. An 8-bit pixel, for example, can be displayed in any of 256 colors (the total number of different configurations that can be achieved by eight 0s and 1s).

pixelation / pixellization The term used to describe an image that has been broken up into square blocks resembling pixels, giving it a "digitized" look.

plug-in Software, usually developed by a third party, that extends the functionality of another piece of software. Plug-ins are common in image-editing and page-layout applications. Numerous filter plug-ins are available for Photoshop, offering a range of visual stylings and effects not availble in the main program.They are also common in Web browsers for such features as playing movies and audio.

PNG Portable Network Graphics. A file format for images used on the Web that provides 10–30% "lossless" compression, and supports variable transparency through "alpha channels," cross-platform control of image brightness, and interlacing.

posterize / posterization To divide, by photographic or digital means, a continuous-tone image into either a predefined or arbitrary number of flat tones. Also known as **tone separation**.

progressive JPEG A digital image format used primarily for displaying JPEG images on webpages. The image is displayed in progressively increasing resolutions as the data is downloaded to the browser. A cloudy image appears on the screen, which clears as more data is downloaded. Also called "proJPEG."

portrait format An image or page in a vertical format. Also called "upright format."

raster image An image defined as rows of pixels or dots.

raster(ization) Deriving from the Latin word "rastrum," meaning "rake," the method of displaying (and creating) images employed by video screens, and thus computer monitors, in which the screen image is made up of a pattern of several hundred parallel lines created by an electron beam "raking" the screen from top to bottom at a speed of about one–sixtieth of a second. An image is created by varying the intensity of the beam at successive points along the raster. The speed at which a complete screen image, or frame, is created is called the "frame" or "refresh" rate.

render In 3D animation, the term usually refers to wrapping a surface texture over a three-dimensional body, created as a "wireframe," to create realistic-looking objects and landscapes. In Photoshop, however, the Render filters create effects such as clouds and lighting effects, which, when used judiciously, can add realism to, or improve, an image.

rescale Amending the size of an image by proportionally reducing its height and width.

resolution (1) The degree of quality, definition, or clarity with which an image is reproduced or displayed, for example in a photograph, or via a scanner, monitor screen, printer, or other output device.

resolution (2) Refers to monitor resolution and screen resolution. The number of pixels across by the number down. The three most common resolutions are 640 x 480, 800 x 600, and 1,024 x 768.

retouching Altering an image, artwork, or film to modify or remove imperfections. Can be done using mechanical methods (knives, inks, and dyes) or digitally, using Photoshop.

RGB (red, green, blue) The primary colors of the "additive" color model—used in video technology (including computer monitors), or in graphics (Web and multimedia, for example) that will not ultimately be printed by the four-color (CMYK) process method.

rich media A loose descriptive term for websites or Web elements that use technology more substantial than that offered by GIF Animation and simple JavaScript routines. Flash, Shockwave and streaming video are amongst the features that are collectively described as rich media.

rollover The rapid substitution of one or more images when the mouse pointer is rolled over the original image. Used extensively for navigation buttons on webpages and in multimedia presentations.

saturation The variation in color of the same tonal brightness from none (gray), through pastel shades (low saturation), to pure color with no gray (high saturation, or "fully saturated"). Also called "purity" or "chroma."

scan(ning) An electronic process that converts a hard copy of an image into digital form by sequential exposure to a moving light beam, such as a laser. The scanned image can be manipulated by a computer or output to separated film.

scanned image An image that has been recorded by a scanner and converted into a suitable form for reproduction, such as film or digital file.

tag Formal name for a formatting command in HTML (and other mark-up languages). A tag is turned on in HTML listings, for example, by placing inside angle brackets and then turned off again by adding a forward slash. For example to type the word webpage in bold text would use the command <bold>webpage</bold>.

text path An invisible line, either straight, curved, or irregular, along which text can be forced to flow.

thumbnail A small representation of an image used mainly for identification purposes in an image directory listing or, within Photoshop, for illustrating channels and layers. Thumbnails are also produced to accompany PictureCDs, PhotoCDs and most APS and 35-mm films submitted for processing.

TIFF, TIF Tagged Image File Format. A standard and popular graphics file format originally developed by Aldus (now merged with Adobe) and Microsoft, used for scanned, high-resolution, bitmapped images and for color separations. The TIFF format can be used for black-and-white, grayscale, and color images, which have been generated on different computer platforms.

tile, tiling Repeating a graphic item and placing the repetitions side by side in all directions so that they form a pattern.

tween(ing) A contraction of "in-between." An animator's term for the process of creating transitional frames to fill in-between key frames in an animation.

Uniform Resource Locator (URL) The unique address of every webpage on the Web. Every resource on the Internet has a unique URL, which begins with letters that identify the resource type, such as "http" or "ftp" (determining the communication protocol to be used), followed by a colon and two forward slashes. After this comes the "domain name" ("host"), which can have several parts to it, then, after a slash, the directory name followed by path names to any particular file. Usually if a file name is not stated, the browser will default to the file name "default.html," "default.htm," "index.html," or "index.htm," which is usually the location of the home page.

unsharp masking (USM) A traditional film-compositing technique used to increse the perceived sharpness of an image. This can be achieved digitally in Photoshop.

vector A mathematical description of a line that is defined in terms of physical dimensions and direction. Vectors are used in drawing packages and Photoshop to define shapes (vector graphics) that are position- and size-independent.

watermarking The technique of applying a tiled graphic to the background of a webpage, which remains fixed no matter what foreground materials scroll across it. Images can be watermarked digitally with a copyright notice to minimise theft of copyrighted material, and some sound storage formats can also be watermarked inaudibly to prevent piracy.

web authoring The process of creating documents (usually in HTML or XML format) suitable for publishing on the Web.

webpage A published HTML document on the World Wide Web, a linked collection of which forms a website.

Web-safe A set of colors that will not change when an image is optimized for the Web.

website The address, location (on a server), and collection of documents and resources for any particular interlinked set of webpages.

World Wide Web (WWW) The term used to describe the entire collection of Web servers all over the world, which are connected to the Internet. The term also describes the particular type of Internet access architecture which uses a combination of HTML and various graphic formats, such as GIF and JPEG, to publish formatted text that can be read by Web browsers. Colloquially termed simply "the Web."

Index

Useful Websites and Books

Photoshop sites
www.adobe.com
www.photoshop-café.com
www.grafx-design.com
www.mccannas.com/pshop

Website design and inspiration
www.defytherules.com
www.smashstatusquo.com

Stock photography
www.corbis.com
www.stockbyte.com
www.photodisc.com
www.cadmium.co.uk

Colours
html-color-codes.com
www.visibone.com

Fonts
www.fontshop.com
www.fontmonster.co.uk
www.garagefonts.com

GIF animations
www.animationfactory.com
www.animation-central.com

Photoshop plug-ins
www.plugins.com/plugins/photoshop
www.alienskin.com
www.andromeda.com
www.fractal.com
www.extensis.com
www.xaostools.com

Books
• *Photoshop, Elements and Web Design*
• Adobe Creative Team, *Adobe Photoshop 6 and Illustrator 9.0: Advanced Classroom in a Book*, Adobe Press, San Jose, California, 2001.
• Baumgardt, Michael, *Adobe Photoshop 6.0 Web Design*, Adobe Press, San Jose California, 2001.
• Evening, Martin, *Adobe Photoshop 6.0 for Photographers*, Focal Press, Oxford, 2001.
• Joss, Molly, *How to do Everything with Photoshop Elements*, Osborne/McGraw Hill, Berkeley, California, 2001.
• Lee, Lisa, *Adobe Photoshop 6 Digital Darkroom*, Prima Publishing, Rosewood, California, 2001.
• *Digital Photography and Manipulation* (featuring Photoshop)
• Ang, Tom, *Silver Pixels*, Argentum, London, 1999.
• Daly, Tim, *Digital Photography Handbook*, Argentum, London, 1999 (reprinted 2000).
• Freeman, Michael, *Complete Guide to Digital Photography*, Silver Pixel Press, Rochester, NY, 2001.
• Joinson, Simon, *The Digital Photography Handbook*, Metro Books, London, 1998 (reprinted 2001).

Acknowledgments

I'd like to thank my wife Gill, and my children David and Sarah for their patience through the production of this book and for allowing themselves to be photographed. This book is for you.